THE YEAR
OF THE END

THE YEAR
OF THE END

A Memoir

Anne Theroux

ICON

Published in the UK in 2021
by Icon Books Ltd, Omnibus Business Centre,
39–41 North Road, London N7 9DP
email: info@iconbooks.com
www.iconbooks.com

Sold in the UK, Europe and Asia
by Faber & Faber Ltd, Bloomsbury House,
74–77 Great Russell Street,
London WC1B 3DA or their agents

Distributed in the UK, Europe and Asia
by Grantham Book Services, Trent Road, Grantham NG31 7XQ

Distributed in Australia and New Zealand
by Allen & Unwin Pty Ltd,
PO Box 8500, 83 Alexander Street,
Crows Nest, NSW 2065

Distributed in South Africa
by Jonathan Ball, Office B4, The District,
41 Sir Lowry Road, Woodstock 7925

Distributed in India by Penguin Books India,
7th Floor, Infinity Tower – C, DLF Cyber City,
Gurgaon 122002, Haryana

ISBN: 978-178578-739-3

Typeset in Sabon by Marie Doherty

Printed and bound in Great Britain
by Clays Ltd, Elcograf S.p.A.

for Marcel and Louis

Truth becomes fiction when the fiction's true;
Real becomes not-real when the unreal's real.

Dream of the Red Chamber
Cao Xueqin

This memoir is based on the diary I kept during 1990, the year that my first marriage came to an end. Some time after that, in the late nineties, I used the diary to trigger thoughts and recollections which I wrote down while the events of that year were still fresh in my mind. I was trying to write truth, not fiction.

Actual diary entries and quotations from written sources have been reproduced without alteration, though they may have been shortened. Many of the interviews (with Barbara Cartland, Kingsley Amis and Elisabeth Frink, for example) were transcribed from my cassette recordings. Other conversations are from memory. Names of some minor characters have been changed.

Contents

Contents

Chapter 1

Once upon a time ...

O nce upon a time in a warm December, when I was teaching at a school near Mount Kenya and wondering whether I should pack my bags and drive to Uganda to get married, I bought a diary for the year ahead. Inside the cover was a green, sticky-backed label made up of perforated strips, to be inserted in the diary, ready-printed with these reminders:

Tomorrow is my father's birthday
Tomorrow is my mother's birthday
Tomorrow is my wedding anniversary
Tomorrow is …
Tomorrow is …

When my fiancé came to visit me, wearing a dusty suit, open-necked shirt and plimsolls, having driven 500 miles from Kampala in a day, on a road that was still not completely tarmacked, he seized the diary and the green labels with delight.

'It's a poem by T.S. Eliot,' he said, reading it aloud in a lugubrious voice.

I don't remember sticking the strips into the diary. It was for the year 1968, the year of *les événements* in Paris and the Battle of Grosvenor Square in London, the year of the Tet Offensive, the Biafran War, the Soviet invasion of Prague, the murder of Martin Luther King and the year my first son was born in Mulago Hospital, Kampala on 13th June. None of these could have been marked in advance with a green sticker. And I no longer have that diary. However, I do have a diary for another, much later year, which often opens at this page:

18th January 1990

Paul left today at 8am.

~

We had been married just over 22 years.

The previous evening we had gone out to eat at a local restaurant, where we drank champagne and reminisced. In a short story which he wrote about that final evening of a marriage, the central characters talk wittily and poignantly about the explorer Sir Richard Burton and the sad, misunderstood wife who burnt his books.* The reality was different: we talked about the au pair girls who had cared for our sons while I went out to work and he wrote, and the *amahs* who had done the same job in Singapore. (In Africa they are called *ayahs*, but since we left Uganda when our first son was only four months old, we never employed one.) The conversation chronicled the years.

In 1968, a violent incident in Kampala prompted Paul to resign from his job at Makerere University and make plans to leave Africa. The poet D.J. Enright, Professor of English at Singapore University, was an admirer of my husband's writing and offered him a post as a lecturer. Just before we were due to leave Uganda, the Vice Chancellor, a top man in Singapore's ruling party, discovered that some of this writing might be considered seditious and tried to get the appointment blocked. Dennis Enright threatened to resign. We waited nervously in Kampala; we had no money and nowhere else to go. A compromise was reached: Paul was offered a job on the lowest possible salary and on condition he promised not to write about

---

* 'Champagne' in *My Other Life*, by Paul Theroux, 1996.

Singapore politics. He accepted. We lived in Singapore from 1968 until 1971.

During most of the Singapore years I taught English too, at Nanyang, the Chinese language university, where the students had Chinese names, wore conservative clothes, and were more likely (I suspected) secretly to sympathise with Mao Zedong and the Cultural Revolution than their English-educated counterparts with whom Paul studied the plays of Shakespeare and his contemporaries, and who had names like Annabel Chan and Reggie Chew. To enable us both to do our jobs, we shared our small house off Bukit Timah Road first with Ah Ho, a soft-faced Cantonese girl who left when she had a child of her own, and then with Susan, a svelte Hakka in black stretch-pants. On one very special occasion Susan came out of her room ready for the weekend in a short skirt. 'You got legs!' remarked Marcel, who at eighteen months had the glottal stops of the Singapore Chinese. When Louis was born in 1970, a careworn woman, whose very name, Ai Yah, was like a cry of despair, was recruited as additional help.

I suppose I wouldn't recognise them now. We said good-bye to Singapore in November 1971, taking a final picture of Susan and Ai Yah holding the children, and flew to England. After a brief attempt at rural domesticity in Dorset, we moved to London.

In 1972, when Paul was writing *Saint Jack*, his revenge on the Singapore authorities, and I started work for the BBC, a north-country lass called Beryl moved into our terraced house in Catford; she was a latter-day Beatles fan but also liked the Bay City Rollers, the Jackson 5 and The Osmonds; Marcel and Louis, aged four and two, appreciated her taste in music and the house rang with shrill voices singing 'I'll be your long-haired lover from Liverpool'. Beryl was a good companion when my husband left on his first long absence – a term teaching at the university of Virginia. I had ordered a carpet for the hall. When it was laid, the living room door wouldn't open. Beryl helped me remove the door from its hinges and held it while I sawed half an inch off the bottom. A few weeks later she comforted me when I cried because rain had leaked through the roof and stained the new carpet. I was crying because I found it hard to do my job and run the household without my husband, because I was ashamed of my own weakness and because our home, the first we had owned, was flawed. I wanted it to be perfect.

At Christmas I flew with the children to Virginia to be reunited with Paul. He confessed to an affair with a student, the first admitted infidelity, and I kissed him and said it didn't matter, thinking this was true. We came back to London with a record player for Beryl, but the goodwill was marred when we found evidence of an unruly party held in our living room the previous night. Shortly afterwards Beryl left and her place was taken by a Norwegian girl called Inge, who broke the hearts of several local youths and seduced my young brother-in-law when he came to stay.

Inge was still with us when Paul went off on *The Great Railway Bazaar* journey, which was the beginning of his success as a writer. It was my turn to be unfaithful, and Inge shopped me when he returned. I had confessed myself, but she added further incriminating details. We span into a turmoil of misery and rage which Paul described much later in his novel, *My Secret History*. Miraculously we emerged, not unscathed but ready to resume a fairly happy family life. Inge was succeeded by a Welsh girl called Liz who became pregnant by a local fireman: her family made a day trip to London for the wedding. I think the next was Catherine, a lively seventeen year old who was soon part of the family. There was an Australian called Amy who ordered Louis to stand in the corner when he made a puking face at the food on his plate and a butcher's daughter called Priscilla who entertained him by counting the planes that flew over our house. (By this time we had moved to a bigger house, in Wandsworth, and were on the flight path to Heathrow.) There was another Australian, Sue, who stayed twice, the second time with the man she married (many years later we visited them in New South Wales) and another English girl, Avril, who boiled her jeans in a saucepan used for stew and gave us all diarrhoea. And there was a German, Monika, who had a little dog called Idéfix, and who, in return for some favour which I have since forgotten, painted our bedroom purple.

In the last six or seven years there had been no au pairs, only daily cleaners: Mrs Bondy, Flora Jeffreys and Maisie Flynn. Mrs Bondy had the gift of the memorable phrase and contributed at least two to the family vocabulary: 'They don't have our clean ways' (applied to anyone who lived east of Calais) and 'Having a good pick then?' (addressed to a child furtively fumbling with his nose). She left after a row when the central heating thermostat was mysteriously turned to *max 24 hrs* while we were on a skiing holiday. Flora Jeffreys left to run a canteen on a building site. Maisie Flynn died in St Thomas' Hospital.

We talked about some, but not all of these memories over our last dinner, summoning up a procession of ghosts with mops and brooms. Back in the purple bedroom, having walked home across Wandsworth Common, we made love, as we had done a thousand times before, kissed and turned to our separate pillows. In the morning Paul called a taxi. When it arrived, he sat on the bed and hugged me and we both shed tears.

'I'll be back,' he said. Then he left for ever.

My diary entry reads:

Paul left today at 8am, the beginning of a six-month separation. I spent a futile, miserable day drinking, smoking a joint (I even burnt the carpet) and hoping I can pull myself together tomorrow.

Tomorrow is ...

Chapter 2

August 1989

August 1989 was spent as usual on Cape Cod, in the house Paul had bought in 1983. It was a beautiful house set in three acres of land. The living room had windows on every side and to the north looked out on the long, curved bay, between Plymouth and Provincetown, that forms the inner crooked arm of the Cape. We were in East Sandwich, near the elbow, just a few miles from the Cape Cod Canal and a lighthouse, which glowed at night and hummed a warning. I used to listen to it as I lay in bed next to him.

Neither of our sons was with us that year. They were both in France at a summer school near Montpellier. Marcel would be joining us before the end of the month and then staying on in America: he had a scholarship to Yale to do an MA in International Relations. Louis would not be visiting the Cape this summer: after France he was joining the family of a school friend in Corfu, then returning to London briefly before going up for his second year at Oxford. Paul was moody and distracted, disappointed that our sons had chosen to be elsewhere. But I was there; couldn't we enjoy at last some time alone together?

This year I was not going to collect material for radio programmes as I had during the last few summers. The obvious subjects in the area had been exhausted. I had made a half-hour programme about American attitudes to Ireland, commuting to Boston every day to interview Irish Americans from all points on the political spectrum and spending many hours waiting in vain for Edward Kennedy and Tip O'Neill to return my calls. I had investigated the history of the Native Wampanoag people and interviewed their medicine man, Slow Turtle, aka John Peters ('my slave name' he called it); I had been out on a whale-watching trip and talked to Captain 'Stormy' Mayo about whales and whaling. I had written to Stephen King in Maine, telling him how much I admired his books and asking for an interview; his secretary had politely refused.

This summer I would do nothing but swim in the pool, sunbathe, read and see if I could enjoy being a wife. Perhaps I would make beach plum jelly. This time-consuming and unrewarding activity epitomised for me the life of a housewife on Cape Cod. 'What would I do? Make beach plum jelly?' I asked, when Paul talked about living there permanently. He already spent more time in East Sandwich than I wanted, leaving London in June and not returning till September. The rest of us joined him for the month of August. It was a good place for a holiday but it was a hard place to live in properly, unless you were a professional writer like Paul, who carried his work around with him. If, like me, your well-being depended on having a job to go to, people to talk to, streets to walk through and buses to hop on, more than a month on the Cape began to feel like deprivation.

It was a good place for a holiday, for those who are good at holidays. We had different views on them. For me, being on holiday means filling each day with pleasure and taking a break from duty, preferably in the company of the people you like best. Paul never took a break from writing, perhaps because it *was* his greatest pleasure; only when inspiration failed him, sometimes by lunch time but often not until the light was fading at the end of the day, would he leave his desk and be ready for a walk on the beach, a visit to the cinema, a drink or a conversation. When these quotidian activities seemed inadequate, we would drive the jeep, with his rowing boat swinging dangerously on the trailer behind it, to distant points on the Cape and he would push off for several hours' solitary rowing. I would drive the jeep back home and wait for a phone call late in the evening to let me know where I should pick him up.

Just occasionally he could be tempted to join in the kind of family outing I associate with holidays. A favourite destination for such a trip was Martha's Vineyard, the fashionable island south of the Cape where many famous people had summer homes. We would leave early in the morning with the boys and meet up with other members of Paul's family at the ferry in Hyannis. On board we drank coffee out of styrofoam cups and ate doughnuts, while the boat chugged across the stretch of water which separated the island from the mainland. In Vineyard Haven we rented bicycles for the day and set out along the cycle track to Edgartown, where we would look around the shops and buy sandwiches for lunch, before wheeling our bikes aboard another tiny ferry to the island of Chappaquiddick, even more remote, less populated and more exclusive. It was always hot and by this time the boys would be wearing long-sleeved shirts to protect their arms from the sun while they cycled.

A narrow road through pine trees became a sandy path and eventually we arrived at the bridge where, late one night in 1969, Senator Edward Kennedy's car veered into the water, drowning Mary Jo Kopechne. The Senator, according to his own account, 'dove and dove repeatedly' to save her. We had inspected the site and formed our own conclusions about what really happened, and each year, Paul's brother, a Washington lawyer, would make us huddle round him to hear the latest rumoured version.

'There was another woman in the car.' Gene mouthed the words almost silently into the summer air as we widened our eyes and gripped our handlebars. 'Mary Jo was asleep in the back seat.' He did his best to provide a new piece of gossip each year, though we had long ceased to believe him. This one was too implausible even to pass on at dinner parties in London.

A little further on was our favourite beach, where we would spend the middle hours of the day, swimming, talking and eating our sandwiches.

We usually started the return cycle ride just a bit later than was sensible; the children would be tired and there seemed to be more uphill stretches on the way back, so for the last mile everyone was under pressure to pedal hard, otherwise we would miss the ferry. By the time we got back to the Cape I felt sunburnt, exhausted and satisfied.

There had been variations on the trip. Once, having hired our bikes, we had set out not to Edgartown but to the Gay Head cliffs, on the other side of the island. The cliffs were made of clay with special healing properties and the area had once been inhabited by Native American whale hunters. It was a much longer ride than we had bargained for and when we got to the cliffs, about which I remember nothing, it was time to start back again, with a snatched lunch from a roadside café and no chance of even a swim. The photographs taken during that day show a happy group setting out and a very cross one returning. On another occasion, when Louis was too young to ride a bike, he sat on Paul's crossbar and at a bumpy point on the ride got his foot caught in the spokes, bringing bike and riders crashing to the ground. We made for the nearest beach and bathed his bruised foot. It could have been worse.

But this year, the summer of 1989, Paul and I went to the Vineyard alone and for the first time rented not bicycles but a small motor scooter, which Paul drove while I rode pillion, just as we had once driven round a Pacific island off Tahiti. There was time to explore new areas; time to re-visit the Gay Head cliffs. We strolled on a beach on the far side of the island.

'Look,' said Paul. 'There's a man with no clothes on.'

I squinted into the sun and ascertained that this was so, and that further along the beach there were many naked people. We walked among them, wondering at the different shapes and sizes of men's genitals, classifying them as tassels, bath plugs, carrots and bananas.

'I think they're all the same when they're erect,' I said.

'How do you know?'

'I read it in a book.'

'I don't believe it.'

I agreed it seemed unlikely.

Eventually we took off our clothes and swam. From the water we noticed people higher up the beach rolling in mud and smearing themselves with it. We tried it ourselves and I took a photo of Paul, naked and neanderthal, streaked with clay, which later we stuck on the fridge in the kitchen.

The only thing which marred the day was that I burnt my leg on the engine of the bike. It seemed a trivial hurt at the time, but it got worse as the holiday continued and the burn blistered and oozed.

There was something else hurting me too. That summer Paul had published a book called *My Secret History*, a novel, drawing on our life together, and I was wounded by it. Although there were things about the character based on me which I liked and accepted, Jenny Parent had other qualities which I hated: she was shrewish and humourless. The portrayal diminished me.

I was also upset by the descriptions of Andre Parent's affair with a woman called Eden. In real life this woman was an English teacher from Pennsylvania with whom Paul had had two affairs, one in 1982 and one in 1986. These affairs, unlike previous ones, had been serious: he considered leaving me, hesitating, sulking and making me unhappy and insecure. Both had eventually ended, after much misery, and I had learned to suppress the mad, jealous questions with which I had once bombarded him. The book, cruelly, teased me with answers which may or may not have been fictional. Had he really taken her on one of his trips to India? Had he really ...?

'It's a novel,' said Paul. 'It isn't true.'

The previous year, when I read the book in manuscript, I blue-pencilled certain passages and added phrases in other places, most of which he ignored. I wasn't altogether surprised; some of the additions were written in facetious rage, for instance, 'She was wearing big baggy bloomers' in a scene where the hero undressed his lover. Now that the book had been published, and received good reviews, I had decided that the only way to deal with my discomfort was to go along with Paul's insistence that the whole thing was a work of fiction, which of course it was, in a way. Friends would telephone and ask, 'How did you feel about Paul's book?'

'I think it's a wonderful book.'

There would be a pause. This wasn't the answer they expected. How the conversation continued depended on the degree of their insensitivity, animosity, or nosiness.

'But the wife is such a horrible character,' said one old friend. 'Not at all like you, of course.'

'I quite like the wife. But it's all made up. It's a novel.'

It was hard for those friends who genuinely wanted to sympathise to say the right thing; there was no right thing to say. The book was a betrayal.

The trip to Martha's Vineyard, barbecues with Paul's family (after more than twenty years they were my family too), a visit to Florida including a tour of Ernest Hemingway's house (I have a photo of Paul in Papa's WC), even the prospect of Marcel joining us in a week or two, could not silence the voice shouting in my head: 'No. This is too much.'

One day Paul received a letter from a friend saying what a fine book *My Secret History* was, but how difficult its publication must be for me. He showed me the letter and for the first time seemed to want to know how I felt.

'It is very hard,' I said. 'Sometimes I feel unhappy and afraid about the future.'

I hoped for reassurance.

'Sit down,' he said. 'I've been meaning to tell you something.'

I knew what that meant. We'd been there before. I said it first.

'There's someone else.'

There was a long pause and the sound of wild horses exerting their best effort.

'Yes. But it isn't serious. I told her,' he said with some pride, as if he expected me to be pleased, 'that this had happened before, and that when I had to choose, I chose you.'

'So it's not *her* again?'

'No.'

'So who is it?'

'Why do you need to know?'

'Did you tell her you loved her?'

'I may have done. But it wasn't true.'

The mad, jealous questions and evasive answers began again. Much of what he told me then, later turned out to be untrue.

Feeling that I had been punched hard on an old wound, I went and sat in the toilet to be alone.

Later that day we drove to Boston to meet Marcel's flight. Neither of us spoke for over an hour. As we entered the airport parking lot, he said, with a pathetic attempt at lightness, 'Are you wishing that you'd had an affair too?'

'No. I'm not wishing that. I was thinking that this probably really is the end.'

As he got out of the jeep he was crying.

Over the next few days we behaved as normally as we could, buying clothes and a duvet for Marcel's first term at Yale, cooking and eating together as usual, visiting relatives, even taking a cycle trip along the Cape Cod Canal. If he had said then, or at any time in the next months, the next years perhaps, 'I will always love you. This will never happen again,' I would have done almost anything to keep us together.

He was about to leave for a two-month trip in Australia and New Zealand, the first stage of his research for *The Happy Isles of Oceania*, and we agreed to decide nothing before this was over. He said he wouldn't see the woman during that time. He had told me that she lived in Los Angeles. He would travel to Australia without stopping there. I flew back to London; Paul drove Marcel to Yale and then set out on his journey.

During the two months that followed, he telephoned me many times at great expense to tell me that he loved me and sent me loving letters too, but he never said what I wanted to hear.

Other things were not going my way. I had returned to England looking forward to getting back to work. (I had given up my BBC staff job just over a year ago and was working as a freelance broadcaster.) Among the post I opened on the first day back was the new rota for the Radio 4 arts programme which I had been presenting regularly since the beginning of the year. My name was on it only twice over the next four months. When I telephoned to check, it became clear that I might not be needed at all the following year. Though this was not spelt out, I got the impression they had found another woman presenter to join the team and that they liked her better than me. Another rejection. The future looked bleak, professionally and personally.

Sometimes I behaved destructively, drinking too much and not eating. At other times I tried to be sensible: I spent a long weekend at a health farm (I still use the make-up they recommended) and I contacted the psychoanalyst who had worked with Paul and me three years before when we nearly separated because of the English teacher in Pennsylvania. She agreed to see me on my own. I still have the notes I wrote after the sessions, stored in my old Amstrad: *Dr P suggested I'm not allowing myself to experience the full range of feelings because I exclude those which don't seem useful or sensible. But I don't know what I really do feel, except pain …*

It goes on for page after anguished page – embarrassingly self-pitying to read now, but true at the time … some of the time. I listed all my stored-up grievances against Paul in an attempt to expel the anger the analyst said I was repressing, writing them down in the heat of rage. Now, reading them back, many of them seem petty: *developing rival symptoms when I was ill; not helping enough with preparations when people came to dinner; being too tired to be supportive when I was in labour.* When I came home from the hospital with Marcel, *he didn't look after me. On the Sunday he didn't even get my lunch. When we flew back from Singapore to London, he just slumped on the bed in the hotel, leaving me to cope with the children. In Dorset I used to get up at 5 or 6, get breakfast for the kids, spend the whole day looking after them, getting meals, washing nappies. Once I was so angry I threw a bowl of cereal over his head. He never let me forget it. When I tried to tell him how unhappy I was, he said he had a book to finish.* Sounds as though I was a pain in the arse.

My perspective has shifted. At the time I dragged up anything from the past that backed up the contention that Paul was a villain. There was plenty of evidence. So why did I want him to stay? *Did* I want him to stay? In this crisis, as in our falling in love and in our marriage, there were forces at work which I did not fully understand, however hard I struggled.

Today I had an illumination. I don't want to end my relationship with Paul; I want to end the marriage. I want to get rid of the externally imposed restrictions and attitudes, the stereotypes of wronged wife, nagging wife, indulgent wife/mother and have my own life in my own house – which Paul will enter when it suits us both, not by right. I don't hate Paul – I don't believe the bitter things I wrote earlier.

My feelings were powerful and confused. I tried to simplify them and look at my choices. I could cut my losses and face up to life without Paul; I could embark on a battle with my latest rival (whom I could probably see off, as I had seen off the woman from Pennsylvania); or I could put up with the situation as it was, suppressing the knowledge that Paul would make love to this other woman, or a different 'other woman' when it suited him. None of these seemed right. Part of the trouble was that I didn't know what Paul wanted.

He arrived back in London a few days before my 47th birthday, and for a while we resumed our life as if it were unthinkable that it should end. So much of the way we lived together was enjoyable and comfortable that I couldn't believe he would want to give it up. And yet his infidelity and his uncertainty seemed to spring from a profound dissatisfaction with his life as it was: with London, with me, with the life stage he had reached, the father of sons about to take off on their own, leaving him behind.

During the last months of 1989, every evening on television, we watched the familiar world order shift before our eyes as communism crumbled in Eastern Europe. Our domestic life was also on the brink of collapse and we made a number of changes in a last-ditch effort to shore it up. We bought a new car, and new furniture for the living room to replace the second-hand sofa and chairs I had paid £20 for fifteen years earlier. I disposed of the out-of-tune piano which no one played and the collapsible table-tennis table which was stored behind it; these once coveted items had outlived their appeal and were now a source of annoyance. 'When are we going to get rid of that bloody piano?', he would say. 'No one ever uses it,' and I would prevaricate and maybe finger a few bars of 'Für Elise', or another piece remembered from childhood, as a sign that one day I would play the piano again. Now it went – for nothing, to the first person willing to take it away.

We tried again to talk about the future, to list our options together, in the way the psychoanalyst had taught us when we were racked by similar uncertainties three years earlier: to part for ever, to stay together for ever, to spend a year together, to spend a year apart, to spend a year somewhere completely different. In 1986 I had opted to spend a year together. Paul had agreed. Then he had gone on a short trip alone (part of the travels in China described in *Riding the Iron Rooster*) and come back converted. 'I don't want to spend a year together,' he said. 'I want us to spend the rest of our lives together.' That was exactly what I had wanted but hadn't dared ask for. We celebrated by travelling to Tibet, though in his description of the journey in the book, I am not mentioned.

This time, in 1989, my preference was for a year somewhere completely different: why not in the Pacific? I had always intended to accompany him on at least some of the journeys he would make for his next book. This could be our first long trip together, now that the children were grown up and I had given up my BBC staff job. In the past, when it had seemed hard to be left behind, while he explored places that I too longed to see, I had fantasised about a time when we would travel together, believing I could match Robert Louis Stevenson's idea of the perfect mate.

'*I wished a companion to lie near me in the starlight, silent and not moving but ever within touch. For there is a fellowship more quiet even than solitude and which, rightly understood, is solitude made perfect. And to live out of doors with a woman a man loves is of all lives the most complete and free.*'*

But that was Stevenson's dream, and mine, not Paul's.

'Why not a year in Fiji?' I urged, convinced now that this was what I wanted. Far away from pitying eyes, my hurt pride would heal and I would be able to forgive.

---

* *Travels with a Donkey in the Cévennes* by Robert Louis Stevenson, 1879.

'I don't know.' He had just returned from driving Louis to Oxford.

'You said you knew someone who would let his house to us.'

He was silent.

'It would be a base. You could still travel alone when you wanted to. I could collect some programme material.'

Eventually, unable to bear his unexplained reluctance, I yelled at him and shook his arm.

'I'm afraid of you,' he said, and I felt like an ugly monster. Who would want to be married to me?

We agreed on a six-month separation. It was the most either of us could contemplate.

We went to see a lawyer and drew up an agreement. We discussed how to tell my parents, and whether he should leave before Christmas or afterwards. Since I had already invited my parents and my sister's family to spend Christmas with us, we decided it should be afterwards. Louis would be down from Oxford, Marcel would be over from the States, it would be a happy time to remember.

Of course it was horrible. My sister and her husband had been told we were going to separate; I don't know what they said to their children, Sam and Max, who were then nine and six; Marcel and Louis knew only too well that our future as a family was in jeopardy. My parents knew nothing and seemed to enjoy their presents, the turkey and the Queen's speech as much as usual. We played games: Cards in the Hat, Murder in the Dark, The Parson's Cat and a new one which involved throwing dice and eating chocolate very quickly with a knife and fork as soon as you got two sixes; when the next person threw two sixes they had the right to take over the knife and fork and the chocolate. Inevitably this last game grew rough; Paul and my sons became over-enthusiastic (eager to win, I think, rather than eager to eat chocolate) and the youngest child, my six-year-old nephew, ended up in tears, while my sister tried not to be angry and my parents maintained a tactful silence. I shouted at Paul and my sons and we all felt ashamed.

Also on 25th December 1989, the Ceauşescus were executed by a firing squad.

For the difficult days between Christmas and New Year, I had planned a final trip for Paul and me – a visit to Florence. It was a last attempt to share my world, the best of Europe, at a time when he talked of wilderness and distant oceans. On one of the very last days in December we walked arm in arm through the Boboli Gardens and he said, 'I'm beginning to feel there may be hope for us.'

'I don't think so.'

'Why? Do you hate me?'

'No, I don't. But I despise you.'

He breathed in sharply and walked ahead of me down a flight of stone steps between two rows of conifers. I ran after him and took his arm.

'Don't be sad.'

Who said that?

Chapter 3

January 1990

Monday 1st January

In Florence

We woke up late after seeing the New Year in, walked to the synagogue, which was closed, and then to the Michelangelo terrace to take pictures of the city. We talked a little about the future.

The coach collected us from the hotel and took us to the airport and we got home around 9pm.

The trip to Florence was good. Why did I wait so long to go back there?

~

1990 was the only year in my life when I recorded what I did each day in a diary. Other diaries petered out by the end of January. This year I forced myself to write something on every page, though it did not come easily to me, as you can no doubt tell. A whole page at the beginning of January is taken up with a list of the buildings, works of art and artists who impressed me in Florence. It's a good list, considering we were there for only a long weekend. But then it wasn't my first visit.

I had first been to Florence 28 years earlier, when I was nineteen, just before I went to university. Having stayed an extra term at school in order to take the Oxford and Cambridge entrance exams and been offered a place at St Hilda's College to read English, I had eight months to fill. For five of those months I did an extremely tedious clerical job in Senate House, the administrative centre of the University of London, where I earned nine pounds a week which my mother saved for things I would need at Oxford – like a striped blanket, in case the college did not provide enough bedclothes. My parents were extremely proud that I was going to Oxford. My mother lost no opportunity to slip the fact into conversations and for the rest of her life would refer to me as 'my daughter who went to Oxford'. My father was less embarrassingly boastful but just as pleased. But I knew that when they were my age, they had both been expected to contribute to the family income, whereas I would be a dependent for the next three years. Earning a little money now, in the months I had free, was the least I could do. So all through the winter and spring I sat at a desk performing mindless tasks (like changing 2d to 2½d on a million postcards) and yawned my way home on the underground from Goodge Street to Tooting Bec.

Fortunately, a former French teacher recommended me for a summer job as a *monitrice* at a holiday home for girls, in Megève, in the Alps; there I spent June, July and August. It was better than Senate House, much better. I was in the mountains, speaking French, hearing cowbells, living away from home. But my duties, though not strenuous, were time-consuming. All day I shepherded reluctant teenagers on mountain walks, watched them flirt and splash at the swimming pool, gave them basic English lessons, played table tennis with them, and after they had gone to bed, sat with the proprietress making appropriate responses to her complaints about her hard life and her *mal au foie*. I earned only pocket money, but saved it all. There was nothing to spend it on.

By the end of the summer I was bursting with energy and the desire to wander far afield, in search of things that would be even more useful than a striped blanket in the years ahead. I took a train to Rome, spent nearly two weeks there, mostly riding on a Lambretta behind a young Italian, and then moved south to Naples, Pompeii, Capri and Sorrento. There was just enough money left for a few days in Florence on the way back to London. I arrived in the early morning, after a night sitting on the floor of the crowded train from Naples, left my luggage at the youth hostel, drank a black coffee and set out to confront Michelangelo's David, towering over me in the *Piazza della Signoria*. It was a more memorable moment than my first sight of the original, later that day in the crowded Accademia.

Twenty-eight years on, I took a picture of the same statue and another of Paul posing on a plinth outside the cathedral. I tried to make a connection between then and now. In 1962 I was setting out on my adult life; now I was middle-aged. At that time, what I saw seemed to open up new worlds, and I felt my life had limitless possibilities. Now, I looked with recognition rather than surprise at the works of art that had moved me most: the slaves struggling to break out of their marble blocks in the Accademia, the Fra Angelico frescoes in the monks' cells in San Marco, Ghirlandaio's *The Last Supper* in the Ognissanti refectory. They had not lost their power, but my response was tempered by experience.

Friday 5th January

London

Went to an exhibition of 14th-century Italian art at the National Gallery and bought Vasari's Lives of the Artists. *Changed Paul's sweater and my pyjamas* (Christmas presents) *for bigger sizes.*

⌒

Paul used to say that art is long and life is short. It was a quotation his mentor, V.S. Naipaul, had been fond of, and it was one I pretended to mock, though secretly I believed that it was true.

Ars longa, vita brevis.* My education had hammered home the message that while an individual's days are numbered, a book, a building or a painting lives on. These artefacts may not be eternal (*look on these works ye mighty, and despair!*†) but at least they outlive their makers. And the written word is particularly durable. Perhaps that was why I had married a writer: so that he would make a lasting mark for both of us.

Milan Kundera wrote: '*The novelist destroys the house of his life and uses its stones to build the house of his novel.*'‡

Monday 8th January

Paul and I watched The Mosquito Coast *on television. It was better than I remembered, brilliant in parts.*

⌒

I noticed again, as I had when the film version of Paul's novel was first shown, that in the editing some crucial scenes were skimped, which made it difficult to follow. We had visited Belize during the shooting so I knew what a lot of good material had been thrown away, and that many roles, including the character played by the black American actress Butterfly McQueen, had been reduced to mere appearances. How disappointing for the actors, who had thrown themselves into the hurly-burly of making the film in that sticky Caribbean climate, lived their parts for weeks and maybe months, talked proudly to their friends

---

* *Ars longa, vita brevis* is actually a Latin translation of a Greek aphorism by Hippocrates.
† 'Ozymandias' by Percy Bysshe Shelley, 1818.
‡ *The Art of the Novel* by Milan Kundera. Reprinted with permission.

and families about what they were doing and ended up as faces in the crowd, figures glimpsed and then forgotten, insignificant voices with a line or two of dialogue.

The central figures were ourselves at two removes: Harrison Ford as Allie Fox, a character based partly on Paul, and Helen Mirren as the wife and mother who doesn't have a name. At least 'mother' is an admirable person, capable and uncomplaining, not like the bitter wife in *My Secret History*. If people speculated about the originals behind the fictional characters, I didn't mind if they thought this woman was based on me.

Thursday 11th January

Last night we went to see a play about the Mexican artists, Frida Kahlo and Diego Rivera. I enjoyed it because it was imaginatively staged and reminded me of her paintings; also the actress playing Frida looked just like her, with thick, black hair and a vivid face.

⁓

Frida Kahlo married Diego Rivera in 1928, three years after her pelvis had been smashed in a bus accident. She suffered all her life from the pain, her inability to have children and Diego's unfaithfulness. But she produced pictures that have made her one of the best-known artists of the 20th century, transmuting suffering into triumph. We had a postcard of one of Frida Kahlo's paintings pinned to the notice board in the kitchen. It was the self-portrait in which she is wearing the frilled, white headdress of a Tehuana woman, leaving only her face exposed; on her forehead is the image of Diego Rivera. Paul had put the picture there.

I don't know what kind of woman is best suited to be the wife of an artist. There seem to be two extremes: the equally-talented brilliant pair – perhaps Diego and Frida were examples (though he definitely had the upper hand) and the master and the handmaid – James Joyce and Nora Barnacle come to mind (though she was a feisty woman who gave as good as she got). The second combination works best, it seems. And even when gender roles are reversed and the woman is the greater artist (Virginia Woolf, George Eliot), the partner must accept that since they are less talented, they should take pleasure in the role of servant.

I recognised Paul's talent; I had never doubted it, from the evening in Uganda shortly after we met, when he read to me from the manuscript of his second novel, *Fong and the Indians*. *Thank God*, I thought (for I had been read to by writers before), *I don't have to pretend*. Although I never changed my mind, I left a lot to be desired as a handmaid, being too opinionated and argumentative, too hopeful that I had something to offer the world myself, too intent on finding my own satisfactions. The role of nurturer, admiring listener, hostess and maker of beach plum jelly was not one I could play enthusiastically for very long. I insisted on working, as a teacher and then as a radio producer and broadcaster, saying at first that I did it for the money (which was true – we needed my income in the early years of the marriage) but quite unable to give it up, even when Paul was earning enough money for both of us. Looking back, asking where I had gone wrong, I sometimes regretted being stubborn and independent; at other times I believed it was my salvation.

Many years after I had stopped asking this question, long after the marriage finally ended, Paul answered it in an interview: '*Writers choose their wives. They choose them for certain purposes. They need a specific kind of woman – protective and self-sacrificing types… What they want is a secretary, mother, a guardian of the gate.*' I dropped him a note saying '*if you had given me the job description in advance, I wouldn't have applied.*' But then he would never have made this statement in 1967, when we were both at the beginning of our adult lives.

My own ideal is summed up in a rather dull sentence, which I came across in an article I was reading for a seminar on couple counselling: '*The good relationship is not by any means calm and serene, but it is always characterised by at least a try at an honest encounter through which two people get to know more and more about one another **and by an implicit recognition by each that the growth, the security, and the satisfactions of one are as important as the other's.**'**

We would probably all pay lip service to this, while at the same time believing that it's different for an artist; that outstanding talent confers the right to make use of other, lesser human beings. Sometimes, over the years, we did approach my ideal, the partnership based on an equality which has nothing to do with success.

Saturday 13th January

Shopping. Garden centre. Bathroom carpet.
 Marcel's girlfriend came for dinner.

---

* I can't find the source of this helpful quotation and will be grateful to anyone who can provide it.

Sunday 14th January

Marcel returned to America. So sad to see him go.
  Paul and I did some planting and tidying in the garden.

Monday 15th January

I got depressed and angry again and told Paul that if he's going he
must go now.

We had decided to separate for six months, but we hadn't said
when the separation would start. Meanwhile, for the first two
weeks in January, we had behaved as usual, as if everything
were going to carry on. We sat at the table with our sons each
evening; occasionally we were joined by one or more of their
friends, and once by Mr Chen, who had shown Paul and me
round Beijing three years before and had fled from China following the Tiananmen Square massacre.

I was hoping that Paul would change his mind, but I would
not beg him to stay. The suspense was unbearable, so I told him
to go. He said he would leave in a few days.

Tuesday 16th January

Today I drove to Eastbourne for Auntie Nancie's funeral. Rosamond
came with me.

My favourite aunt had died just after Christmas. She was my
mother's younger sister and though she was over 70, her death

was a shock: the family had been expecting her husband, my Uncle Paddy, to die. He had been seriously ill for months. Nancie had a heart attack while she was visiting him in hospital.

My aunt was very different from my tall and anxious mother. Nancie was a small, funny, blonde lady who used to work behind the bar in the pubs she and my uncle ran. When I was little and she stooped to hug me, she smelt of cosmetics with a hint of Guinness and her bosom felt bouncy against my flat chest. She was always smartly dressed and brightly made-up; she laughed a lot and made other people laugh. Since I was eight or nine I had spent holidays in Sussex with her and my cousins. Being in their home always made me feel happy. My parents occasionally hinted at mild disapproval of Nancie and Paddy, who were fond of a drink and a good time. But there was no doubt my mother was very attached to her sister and late in life she had persuaded my father to move from Dorset to Sussex, in order to be near her.

My own sister accompanied me on the drive to the funeral. I tried to talk to her about my separation from Paul. The words were difficult to find.

'There's someone else. No, not the same woman. A different one. I can't go through all that again.' My voice was angry.

'I don't blame you.' Rosamond was sympathetic in a tactfully understated way. Members of my family avoid displaying strong feelings, though that doesn't mean they don't have them.

'I was wondering what I could do to help,' she said. 'I thought maybe you and I could go skiing, but I'm not sure I should leave David and the boys behind.'

'That's a kind thought. But I'm OK.' Putting on a brave face was another family characteristic. 'I'm planning to go to Egypt.'

'Good idea. Haven't you been there before?'

'Only to Cairo. For work. This time I want to take a Nile cruise and visit the Valley of the Kings and the temples of Karnak and Luxor.'

'I'd *love* to do that,' she said wistfully.

That felt better. I was a lucky person after all.

We picked up Mum and Dad and took them to the crematorium.

The service wasn't as moving as it should have been but the hymns were good: 'Jerusalem' and 'Onward Christian Soldiers'. And there was a note in the programme which said 'Sing lustily: Nancie always did!'

I was touched by the way my cousin and her husband stood side by side in the front pew, both rather stout in their winter coats, though she was considerably shorter than him. He held her arm. When I got back to London I described to Paul those two figures, one supporting the other at the time when she most needed it. Might we be able to do that for each other?

The saddest thing that day was my uncle's unplanned appearance at the family gathering after the funeral. It had been agreed between my cousins and the nursing staff of the hospital that he was far too ill to attend; he wouldn't even realise it was taking place.

'Much better,' commented my mother. 'He'd only cry if he came.'

But Paddy had known it was the day of his wife's funeral and had got himself dressed and ready to go. The matron rang my cousin to find out what to do. It was already too late for the service, but someone collected him and brought him to the house, where he sat in his wheelchair with tears in his eyes, surrounded by people fumbling with plates and drinks. One by one we bent down to offer our sympathy, though no one could hear what he said in reply. Two months later he died too.

Three years later my cousin's husband, who had supported her so stoutly and so tenderly, died of a stroke.

Sunt lacrimae rerum. *

Wednesday 17th January

Paul and I went out for a meal and talked about old times, especially all the nannies and au pairs we've had.

We came back and made love.

Thursday 18th January

Paul left today — the beginning of our six-month separation. I cried horribly as he was leaving. He cried too then left in a taxi and I spent a miserable day, drinking, smoking a joint and hoping I can pull myself together tomorrow.

Friday 19th January

Yesterday was a terrible day. In the evening I had a desire to telephone Paul that was too powerful to resist, but no one answered.

Then I smoked a joint so strong that I hallucinated and imagined I heard a person in the hall downstairs. I thought it must

---

* 'There are tears at the heart of things,' or 'Life is tragic.' Virgil's *Aeneid*, Book 1.

be Paul – he'd changed his mind. Then I thought it was a burglar
and screamed down the stairs 'Who's that?' No one answered.
Eventually I collapsed on the bed in the spare room.

Today I felt better.

⁓

Better than the day before, that is. I could hardly have felt
worse.

If I had not kept a diary, I would not remember the days
and weeks that followed his departure. The entries show a busy
and interesting life; my memory is of desolation.

Interviewed David Grossman about his book See Under: Love.

⁓

I regularly presented the books edition of the BBC World Service
arts programme, *Meridian*. This involved reading several books
and interviewing either the author or a reviewer. In the last
week of January, as well as the Israeli writer David Grossman,
I talked to the actress Maria Aitken, who had written a book
about the early travel writer Mary Kingsley, and to Christopher
Frayling about a book on Vlad the Impaler, the real-life model
for Dracula. I also read a biography of Turgenev by Henri
Troyat and an unfinished novel called *The People* by Bernard
Malamud. Five books.

It shocks me to discover that I remember almost nothing
about them, though I read them carefully and with pleasure at
the time. Art may be long, but for those who have poor memories, reading a book is an ephemeral experience, like going to
the theatre or the cinema. Of course you can put the book on

your shelf and return to it and I did that with some of mine. (A check reveals that of the books just mentioned, only Grossman's novel is there; why not the Troyat? Surely I didn't let that go?) Others I sold in the back room of a shop in the Strand. This was a quick business. The man looked at the publication date: if it was less than a month ago, he offered a good percentage of the original price; if it was more, he shoved the book to one side and at the end of the transaction grudgingly added an extra pound or two to the total. The method encouraged decisiveness about what to keep, but sometimes led to mistakes and regrets.

Wednesday 24th January

Interviewed Joan Smith for Men by Women, *the programme I'm doing for Roger.*

⌒

Among my freelance projects was a montage feature pro-gramme in which women talked about men, from birth to death. It was one of a pair of programmes devised and overseen by Roger Fenby. He had done interviews himself for the one called *Women by Men* and commissioned me as interviewer for the companion programme. My present mood made me more responsive to negative views of men than indulgent ones – men were traitors, men took all they could get and broke your heart, men pretended to love women but really wanted to hurt them, men enticed women into cars for sex, then drove off bridges and let them drown – so I enjoyed interviewing the feminist writer Joan Smith, who in her book *Misogynies* explores men's hatred of women, taking the Yorkshire Ripper as a starting point. She told me after the interview that she was planning to write something about men who travel and explore the world: 'I think it's an attempt to get away from their mothers', she said, looking me in the eye. *Or their wives*, I thought, but said nothing.

Joan had a point. Some years later I read a book called *The Problem of the Puer Aeternus*, by Marie-Louise von Franz, which convinced me that many travellers are boys who never grow up, in whom *'all those characteristics that are normal in a youth of seventeen or eighteen are continued into later life, coupled in most cases with too great a dependence on the mother ...'**

Pueri aeterni are charming, enthusiastic and adventurous, but they have a shadow side which is cruel and unfaithful. And because they are escaping from powerful mothers, they are afraid of women. When the going gets too tough for the delightful boy, especially when a woman stands up to him, argues, demands that he face up to his responsibilities, he changes into a brutal man and walks away.

For the same programme, *Men by Women*, I talked to a pregnant woman who was dismissive about her husband's attempts to help around the house: 'He says "I'll clean the bath" but I know there's going to be a rim of dirt round it and I'll have to do it again so what's the point?' She sounded tired, exasperated and afraid. I found it easy to share her indignation. Men were selfish, men tackled chores in a half-hearted way so that they wouldn't be asked to help again, men wanted the pleasure of having children but not the hard work. Of course I didn't say these things, I let her say them.

---

* *The Problem of the Puer Aeternus*, by Marie-Louise von Franz, Inner City Books, 2000.

Wednesday 31st January

Travelled to Dorset to interview Elisabeth Frink for Men by Women.

⌒

There are patterns in life which owe nothing to the devices of art. On the first day of January I had stood in Florence, feeling cold and looking at the statue of David, with his sling resting on his shoulder, his balls resting on his thighs: relaxed and ready to kill. On the last day of the month I walked through Elisabeth Frink's garden, shivering slightly and staring at more naked men: bronze statues who avoided my eyes and looked out over the Dorset countryside.

'A lot of my earlier figures were running men.' (Her words were recorded and used in the programme.) 'They were naked, therefore they were vulnerable. And they were running or flee-ing from some persecution or other, whereas the later nudes are much more sensual in a way. They are nude rather than naked and they are very much more solid characters.'

Her most recent sculptures were based on the Riace bronzes – huge Greek warriors found in the sea a few years earlier, dating from the 5th century BCE, beautiful, but with sinister faces. 'I want to show the male as an aggressive person interlaced with all these vulnerabilities,' she said, explaining that Greek warriors had to fight, whether they wanted to or not. That's what being a warrior meant. 'Some wanted to, some didn't. The Greeks called them heroes, but in fact they were thugs,' she added as an afterthought. She gave both Roger and me illustrated booklets about the sculptures. The picture on the cover, Frink's *Riace IV*, 1989, reminded me of the snapshot of Paul covered in thera-peutic mud on the nudist beach in Martha's Vineyard.

'Should we have asked her to sign them?' asked Roger, as we looked through the booklets on the train back to London.

It had never occurred to me. I wish now that I had.

As well as work, the diary records going to the theatre with friends (*Bent* by Martin Sherman at The National with Jenny; *The Pelican* by Strindberg at a theatre in Notting Hill with Margaret), visits from Louis, my younger son, (he would arrive by coach from Oxford for the weekend) and frequent meals with my sister and her family where I felt comfortable but sometimes sad because my nephews reminded me poignantly of how my own children had been ten years earlier, how I was then – so different from today.

For despite what looked like an enviably absorbing life, I was lonely and bereft. There was the pressure of a stone on my chest, another wedged at the back of my throat and another pushing from behind my eyes, trying to make me cry.

Unhappiness is a physical affliction. I felt sick, I was seldom hungry, my metabolism changed as though the misery had seeped into every cell of my body. I had lost weight. Sometimes I would catch a glimpse of myself in the mirror, a frightened middle-aged woman, with startled eyes and a sad mouth. Often I smoked pot at night so that I wouldn't think dreadful thoughts before I slept. Once I fell asleep with my clothes on. I would often wish, just before I lapsed into unconsciousness, that I would not wake up in the morning.

A small healthy person inside my sad hulk recognised that action was needed to keep me afloat for the next six months. Perhaps travel would do the trick. Give it a go. Start up the engines. I left for Egypt on a package tour two weeks after Paul's departure.

Chapter 4

February

Saturday 3rd February

Egypt

Woke early to find the boat in motion and looked out of my window to see the waters and banks of the Nile — just as I'd imagined it would be! Palm trees, fields, mud buildings and minarets, people washing clothes and pots, fishing, working in the fields; children shouting and waving at our boat.

Visited the Temple of Hathor which was built in the Roman–Egyptian period (Ptolemaic) and has interesting bas reliefs, a horoscope and a famous depiction of Cleopatra with Caesarion, which I think I missed.

～

Breathe a sigh of relief. I am going to summarise the next section of the diary and spare you the details of the tombs of Tutankhamun, Rameses II, Rameses VI (I think), and the temples of Karnak, Luxor, Esna, Kom Ombo and even Abu Simbel. You must take my word that I snapped some brilliant photographs, especially of the temple at Karnak which I went back to on my own because the guide had chivvied us when we made our group visit and I needed more time.

Nor will I transcribe the conversations I had with the fellow travellers on the *Queen Isis* who are listed in my diary, among the ancient monuments. John and Pam had a dry cleaning business in Epsom; Peter was a council building advisor; his wife, Mo, made and sold soft toys; Judy and Maisie were old friends from Nottingham who had slipped away without their husbands; Anne, a legal secretary, was fancied by one of the waiters; her friend Babs, a retired office worker, had a daughter she swore she would never speak to again (I wonder if she has); Isa used to work in television and now ran a hotel in Cumbria.

Until I read the diary, I had not thought about them for years. The names conjure faces, voices, gestures. At the time I felt close to them, a member of the group, glad to have people to talk to and eat with, only slightly concerned that so many of the women had packed enough dresses to wear a different one to dinner every evening. They were generally respectful about the antiquities we visited, but became more animated when they had the chance to haggle in local bazaars. One young couple never left the boat. On the last night of the trip there was a fancy-dress party. I hired a black and gold kaftan and a beaded headdress from the shop on the boat and noted in my diary that it had been 'quite jolly'.

Taking the trip worked. It made me feel better. The ancient culture was both strange and familiar. I was at last really seeing objects I had first encountered in books or films when I was a child. Confirming these images gave enormous pleasure: ah yes, the statues of Memnon, sitting side by side, battered, square and oddly coiffed; yes, Rameses II, looking not unlike Yul Brynner in *The Ten Commandments*. And there were surprises too, especially the wall paintings in the tombs. I had not expected them to be so lively. The people, despite their flatness, looked as real and busy as their descendants on the banks of the Nile.

The great benefit of travel is not in the movement, the miles covered, the frontiers crossed, but in being a stranger in a strange land. Glimpses of other lives can lighten a heavy heart. The size and age of the world made my own misery seem small. When I stood outside the great temple at Abu Simbel and looked south, towards Sudan and Ethiopia, imagining the waters of the Nile winding to their much disputed source, I knew that the whole great continent of Africa was there, waiting to welcome me back. I felt ready to set out with a rucksack.

Could I take these hopes home with me, along with the paintings on papyrus (now hanging in the hall, not too prominently), the silver Coptic cross (resting in my jewellery box) and the very heavy granite cat (sitting in the garden, minus an ear)?

Friday 9th February

The flight back to Gatwick was uneventful. Drank too much.

Saturday 10th February

Woke feeling awful.

Sunday 11th February

Discovered that the skylight had blown off the roof and when I climbed into the attic to try and fix it, part of the ceiling in Marcel's bedroom fell down. Called the roofing company and eventually a man came and did a temporary cover-up job.

Meanwhile, Nelson Mandela was released from gaol. He was very impressive and for once I felt optimistic about the possibility of peaceful change in southern Africa.

⌒

In case it sounds as though the hole in the roof was more important to me than Mandela's liberation, let me explain that I was watching television, waiting for him to appear and I got bored with the commentary and slipped upstairs to make the ill-judged inspection. By the time I was able to watch television again, Mandela was a free man.

The diary entry, as so often, is perfunctory and inadequate. Nelson Mandela had been my hero since the 1950s, when a left-wing Latin teacher had awakened her small sixth-form class to the injustice of South Africa. Our first act of solidarity was to confront the school housekeeper about the oranges served as dessert at dinner. (Dinner was at lunch time in those days.) With two of my friends I made my way behind the serving counter and into the forbidden territory of the hissing, clattering kitchen, where sulky minions prepared uneatable food. The evidence was in our hands.

'Excuse me. Are these oranges from South Africa?'

'Certainly not!' The plump housekeeper surprised us with her vehemence. 'I never buy South African goods.'

Since we had no grounds for organising a boycott of school dinners, we found other ways to demonstrate our commitment. Together we linked arms in Trafalgar Square in 1960, following the Sharpeville massacre. We attended lectures and conferences. We discovered that the South African government was not the only oppressor in Africa; we learned about the struggles for independence going on all over that continent. I made up my mind to work in Africa as soon as I finished my education. That was how I came to spend three years there in the sixties, in some ways the best years of my life. My adolescent idealism may have been naïve, but nothing that has happened then or since has changed my views.

'Friends, comrades and fellow South Africans, I greet you all in the name of peace, democracy and freedom for all.'

Amandla!

Tuesday 20th February

Went to a VSO selection board where I was interviewed and had to engage in group activities like demonstrating the uses of an umbrella and putting ping-pong balls in buckets.

After 25 years, I had made a second application to Voluntary Service Overseas, the organisation which had sent me to Africa in 1965. It was much bigger now, and according to its brochure, willing to consider older people for jobs abroad. There were several of us oldies at the selection day, though most of the applicants were youngsters in their final year of university.

I'd had some experience of jumping through hoops to get jobs, so the selection process didn't faze me, even though this hoop-jumping was more literal than most. In the umbrella exercise I decided to avoid the obvious and made only a passing reference to the function of protection from rain, preferring to stress that it might be used as a boat (as in a well-known Winnie the Pooh story) or to dance with (as in the film *Singing in the Rain*). I can't remember what else I did to demonstrate my suitability for work in a developing country, but two days later I got a letter saying I had been accepted. I tried not to get excited; if Paul and I were reunited, the VSO plan might come to nothing (though in theory there was no reason why he shouldn't accompany me); besides, VSO had to find a suitable posting for me: I had said I wanted to work in radio. But from now on, when I felt at my worst, I would whisper a prayer to any god who might be keeping an eye on abandoned wives: 'Please, let me go back to Africa.' I believed Africa would heal me.

I had been a volunteer in Kenya from 1965 to 1966. My first job after university, my first journey outside Europe, was in one of the most beautiful countries in the world, two years after independence. *Bliss was it in that dawn to be alive. But to be young was very heaven.**

I worked at the Voice of Kenya radio station's schools broadcasting division and also taught at a secondary school in Nairobi. I was disappointed at first that Nairobi was such a big, modern city. My dream was to be in the bush, living in a mud hut, in a little clearing in the jungle, where no one knew I had got a second rather than a first at Oxford and I could help with the farming and teach poetry. However, another more worldly self had seized the pen which filled out the application form and requested work in educational radio. This request, quite surprisingly, had been granted. I shared an office with a young Kenyan teacher called Levinson who had been seconded to the radio station under an Africanisation policy and was resented by some of his European colleagues. When Levinson and I had morning coffee in the staff canteen he always insisted on paying for both of us and always made the same joke when I protested. 'That's African socialism!' It was a phrase coined by President Julius Nyerere in neighbouring Tanzania. I don't remember exactly

---

* William Wordsworth recalls his youthful excitement about the French Revolution, in *The Prelude*.

what African socialism was; for me it will always mean a cup of coffee bought by Levinson.

I soon discovered that I had only to take a short bus ride from the city to find huts, goats, cattle, women pounding grain and all the other emblems of the Africa of my fantasies – plus the smells that still retain their power: damp vegetation, wood fires at night, sweet blossoms in the sun. Kenya in the mid-sixties offered a delicious combination of idealistic satisfaction and pleasure. I fell in love with Africa and was determined to find a way of staying there after my year was up.

During my last months in Nairobi, I applied to a scheme called Teachers for East Africa run by the British Ministry of Overseas Development. I was accepted and moved straight from Nairobi to Kampala to spend a year at Makerere University, doing a Diploma in Education. This should have been followed by two years' teaching, and I had been posted, at my own request, to a school in a small town called Embu, near Mount Kenya. Here I hoped I might realise my dream. However, in the final term of my Dip Ed course, I attended a lecture by a young American with a French-looking name. The lecture was called 'Tarzan is an Expatriate'; in it he attacked the foolish and patronising attitudes of Europeans in Africa – even those who believed they were there to help.

His taunts about 'doing a little good in a warm climate' hit home. His appearance – he wore a white suit, an open-necked shirt and tinted glasses with metal frames – also made an impression. He was the coolest, most handsome man I had ever seen.

A few days later the same young American sat down next to me in the Kampala jazz club and I told him how much I had enjoyed his lecture. He made a date for the next evening. We fell in love. I tried to get my posting changed but it was too late. We met in February 1967. In June I travelled to my school in Kenya while Paul remained in Kampala, where he taught in the extra-mural department of the university. We were 500 miles apart, writing passionate letters, arguing about whether I should give up my job to be with him, about the value of the job – 'What's the point of a British-style education for the elite?' he sneered – and about African politics – 'These politicians are totally corrupt; we shouldn't be supporting them.' In the end I gave in. I agreed to leave Embu, even though it meant breaking my contract after only six months. I would look for a school in Kampala that needed a teacher.

It was painful to give up my job. I knew I was letting down the girls at Embu school. If there was a justification for having a pleasant time in a warm climate, it was delivering the goods: O level passes which would qualify these girls to move on to the sixth form and perhaps university. Education might open doors for them, as it had for me.

One night when I was on dormitory duty, I explained that I was engaged and would soon be married. I would be moving to Uganda to live with my husband. They would have another teacher.

A sympathetic sigh swept the room. Heads were raised from their pillows, heads covered in tiny plaits which would be combed out next morning.

'What is he like, your fiancé?'

'He's an American.'

'An American! Is he handsome?'

'Very.'

'Ah!' another sigh, an approving one, went round the dorm.

'We shall miss you!' said one of the girls, whose name was Florence, though she pronounced it Frolence. 'But we hope you will be very happy.'

'Thank you. I shall miss you. I shall never forget you.'

After I'd turned out the lights, I walked back to my small house, the first I had lived in alone, shining my torch on the ground and my feet squelching in wellington boots. It was the rainy season – the short rains. The air was damp and thick with smells. The night noises of Africa throbbed in my ears.

A few weeks later Paul came to collect me and we drove to Kampala where we were married in the registry office. Paul wore the same white suit he had been wearing when he gave the lecture called 'Tarzan is an Expatriate'. I wore a mini-skirted dress, made in Nairobi from a length of green and blue chiffon intended for a sari. There was more than enough for the dress, even though it was generously cut to allow for the slight bulge of my pregnancy. The dress and the extra length of material are now stored at the bottom of a wooden chest.

We had agreed that when our baby was old enough, I would find a job at a school in Kampala, but a few months after I moved to Uganda we were attacked by demonstrators who stopped our car as we drove into town to shop one Saturday. They were protesting against Ian Smith's illegal regime in Rhodesia. We were strongly opposed to Smith's racist government ourselves, but there was no way they could know this. They smashed the windscreen and stood around the car, yelling abuse and hitting it with sticks and stones until an Indian shopkeeper beckoned us inside to take refuge. Our injuries were insignificant – just a few cuts on my legs from the broken wind-screen – but I was pregnant and frightened and when Paul said he wanted to leave Africa, I didn't object.

'I've had a letter from Dennis Enright,' he told me, as I lay panting in labour in Mulago Hospital. 'He wants me to go to Singapore. What do you think?'

'Sounds OK,' I grunted between contractions. I didn't know much about Singapore but it was hot and foreign, which at that stage in my life was what I wanted. I would never grow to love it in the way I loved Africa.

Paul's novel, *Girls at Play*, first published in 1969, by which time we were living in Singapore, is loosely based on Embu Girls School in Kenya, where I taught. It begins: '*The flame trees enclosed the hockey field in a high leafy wall of bulging green: rotting orangey-red blossoms littered the moist grass.*' It's a lush description, each word carefully selected by a master craftsman, though he was still only in his twenties. The second paragraph starts, '*If the fat black girls had not been there and playing, the order of this playing field in the highlands of East Africa would terrify.*' *Fat*, black girls? The girls I taught were not fat. One or two were, perhaps, but most were quite skinny. And there he goes again: '*For the black, large-buttocked girls at the school there was nothing to worry about. In their green bloomers and gray jerseys which showed their swinging unsupported breasts, they ran heavily hunched and held their sticks low, yelping cheerfully.*'

Excellent description, but please be clear that those are not the girls I taught. Nor are the collection of grotesques who make up the staff of the school anything like the headmistress and teachers I worked with. Well, not really. And yet every once in a while, a detail, a description, a conversation chimes absolutely with my memories in a way which makes the novel very disconcerting for me (though I am not in it, except perhaps as the colourless biology teacher, Pamela Male) and no doubt for others who recognise bits of themselves in the characters.

'*The school and all the girls in this book are fictions,*' says the author's note. '*The landscape is real and so are the girls' passions and attitudes.*' I'm not sure about the last claim. The landscape, yes. The passions and attitudes are real only within the world created by the author, whose note ends by explaining why there are no lessons described in the novel: '*While I am aware that African classroom scenes would make for some pretty lively reading, it would be misleading for me to suggest that the teachers in this book are different from others in Africa.*'

When I read this I was angry.

'That's not fair. I know lots of teachers who are hardworking and conscientious.'

Paul just laughed and wouldn't be drawn. For the first time I had the odd experience of seeing events and people in my life portrayed by Paul. It was wonderfully done, but it wasn't true. I tried to write my own account of Africa but it was slow and clumsy. Competing with my husband as a writer was as futile as trying to emulate the somersaults and backflips of an acrobat. Did this mean that my view of life was of no importance? Certainly not. I resolved that despite being married to such a formidably talented man, I would always look at the world through my own eyes and express what I saw in my own way.

Paul wrote another novel about Africa after *Girls at Play*. *Jungle Lovers* is set in Malawi where Paul had worked as a Peace Corps volunteer before being thrown out for plotting against Hastings Banda. Perhaps because it took place in a country I didn't know and among characters I didn't recognise, I had fewer reservations about it. It also seemed more large-spirited, less misogynistic. The main character marries an African woman and finds happiness. The description of the birth of their child is based on the birth of our son, Marcel.

Wednesday 28th February

Put together Men by Women.

⌒

This was a programme without a guiding narrative voice. Assembling the words and sounds of real life and making a meaningful pattern can be very satisfying. The danger is that the links and associations which make sense to the compiler may not have the same effect on the listener, in which case the programme is a failure. I was working for Roger Fenby, a producer I liked and admired. He had already assembled a programme in which men talked about women; now he was overseeing mine, in which the roles were reversed.

'It'll tell the story of man's life, the stages, the contradictions, but seen through the eyes of women,' he had mused. 'Maybe it could also trace the shape of a man's body. Start with the head (thoughts, ideas) then the heart (feelings, life) then the genitals (sex and reproduction) …'

'Maybe. It should certainly include all those things.'

During the past weeks I had collected the ingredients. I've already mentioned the interviews with Elisabeth Frink, Joan Smith and the pregnant woman whose husband was unhelpful.

A visit to a women's self-defence group had provided actuality of the ladies fending off male attackers, while the teacher encouraged them in a helpful Joyce Grenfell voice: 'He's coming towards you. Now raise your knee sharply!' At Trinity Hospice in Clapham, the matron had talked about the difference between the way men and women died: men found it harder, she said, because they hated being weak so much. And I had interviewed Fiona Richmond, the glamour model and sex symbol, sitting in Eastleigh airport near Southampton, sizing up the passing men and talking about their bums and dangly bits.

After listening to all the tapes and making notes, with double ticks by anything which pleased me, I listed the good parts on index cards and shuffled them around to make an order. Then I cut sections out of the original tapes and assembled them on two spools, so they could be played alternately, one flowing into another. The programme began with a woman preacher saying '*Man born of woman has but a short time to live; like a flower he blossoms and then withers, like a shadow he flees and never stays; in the midst of life we are in death.*' The words were faded under the sound of a baby being born and a woman's voice saying 'It's a boy!' Then followed reflections, by women, on every stage of a man's life: childhood, young adulthood, fatherhood, the many guises of man in his prime, maturity, old age and death. Joan Smith talked about the violent feelings that turned men into rapists. The women's defence group hurled men to the ground. Elisabeth Frink talked about vulnerable thugs and Fiona Richmond added salacious mockery. The matron of the hospice described how men died, a woman talked sadly about the death of her husband, and then the final words of the funeral service, *Ashes to ashes and dust to dust.*

I played the rough cut to Roger, feeling moved by my own work. He clutched his head in a despairing way and my heart sank.

'I didn't like that junction between Fiona Richmond and Elisabeth Frink.'

'But they were both talking about men's bodies …'

'The levels sounded wrong. The Eastleigh airport noise needs to be faded more gradually.'

'I can sort that out,' I said, slightly crossly. 'It's a rough cut.' He was right, of course.

Together we worked on the tapes and by the time we had finished it was a good programme. It was rebroadcast twice and I think Roger still has a copy.

Chapter 5

March

Friday 2nd March

Interviewed Kingsley Amis for the series Ex Libris. *He was very co-operative, talking about his collection of books — many of them on drink (especially whisky) but also quite a few sci-fi books and thrillers.*

~

Ex Libris eventually had its name changed to *Writers' Bookshelves*. The idea was to ask writers to talk about the books they owned, with them actually there in front of us, so that they could take them down, flick through the pages and read extracts. Sir Kingsley Amis gave the interview at the house in Primrose Hill which he shared with his first wife and her third husband. It was a tall, narrow, Victorian house, rather like mine, and he occupied two adjoining rooms on the ground floor – a bedroom (which I didn't see) and a bay-windowed sitting room, lined with bookshelves, with a desk and a manual typewriter which he obligingly demonstrated so that I could record the sound of the writer at work. Then he rose, rather carefully, to show me the books.

'I got rid of a lot and I've had a couple of divorces. And lots of moves.' He sounded regretful. 'It's not a lifetime's collection. It would be pitifully small if it were that. It's what survived; and what I've acquired in the last twenty years or so.'

There was a large collection of science fiction books, a whole shelf of books about whisky and another shelf of books about wine. 'I'm quite strong on drink. That's quite a flourishing department of my library.' Another shelf held cassettes. 'Jazz,' he said, waving at them. 'I play jazz every morning for twenty minutes or so while I'm getting dressed.' Then there was the poetry shelf from which he singled out Auden, Graves and Larkin from the 20th century; Arnold, Tennyson and Browning from the 19th, plus Housman, his favourite. He chose to read a poem which Housman based on lines by Robert Louis Stevenson, ending:

> *'Tis evening on the moorland free,*
> *The starlit wave is still:*
> *Home is the sailor from the sea,*
> *The hunter from the hill.* *

'It's about death,' he said, snapping the book shut.

His taste in fiction was particularly eclectic. Chesterton was a great favourite. So was Ian Fleming and another selected reading was the ending of *Casino Royale* when James Bond reports to HQ in London that his lover has committed suicide.

> *'This is 007 speaking. This is an open line, this is an emergency, can you hear me? Pass this on at once. 3030 was a double, working for Red Land. Yes, dammit, I said was. The bitch is dead now.'*

As he read, Sir Kingsley's voice began to falter and he could hardly say the final words. There may have been a reason why, on this particular day, he was so melancholy. Perhaps some personal loss made his heart strings susceptible to old tunes; perhaps it was intimations of his own mortality.

'At my time of life I do an awful lot of re-reading,' he said. 'I'd like to think there's some new stuff yet to come out that I'll latch onto, but I'm not very hopeful.'

'You don't think much of modern writing?'

---

* 'Home is the sailor', A.E. Housman.

'I feel a bit left high and dry by it. The only one I can see anything in at all is my own son, Martin, and I feel about him, "What is he getting at? What the devil is this young fellow getting at?" But that's what I should be feeling. The others, and I won't mention any names, I can see all too well what they're getting at and it's been done better before.'

Now that was more like it! That was the Kingsley Amis I had expected – crusty, intolerant and mocking, not this other, sorrowful fellow. We looked up at his own books, on a high shelf that he reached by standing on a concordance. He said he was waiting for a copy of the Romanian translation of *Lucky Jim*.

'I like to fantasise that the first thing they did when Ceauşescu was overthrown was to say "Right, now we can publish *Lucky Jim*!"' he chortled. 'But I shan't see the money because they don't send you money from communist countries.' He was starting to get gloomy again, but pulled himself up. 'Perhaps they will now.'

Saturday 3rd March

Went to a St Hilda's meeting which Dawn Adès addressed. She's Professor of Art History at Essex. I felt a failure and rather sad.

～

St Hilda's was my old Oxford college. Dawn had been my contemporary and was now not only a professor, but the author of a number of distinguished books. I was in a mood that particular day to resent and envy the achievements of others, perceiving my failure as the black shadow of their glory. Why did I feel such a failure? When I told people what I had done in my life they found it interesting. It *was* interesting. But it didn't add up to much. And the future was so uncertain. Would I go to Africa, would I continue to freelance, would I look for another job? Up to now I had tried to make the best of whatever situation I found myself in, juggling family life and work. Take away the family life, and the work alone was insubstantial.

I left early to avoid having to talk too much and pretend that everything was fine.

Other diary entries for early March record more books read, more interviews with writers, more theatre and cinema visits, more meals with my sister and her family and a visit to my parents when I told them about the separation from Paul. I had been dreading this so much that I had written in advance stating the facts in order to forestall an emotional response. I noted that '*in the event they were terrific – calm and not nosy at all. I didn't go into any details but intimated it had something to do with my unwillingness to live in America. They seemed to accept this.*'

The next day I collected Louis from Oxford and brought him back to London for the Easter vacation; the day after that I left on a trip to Budapest and Prague with my friend Jenny Hargreaves, who had long-standing links with Eastern Europe and wanted to find out how her friends felt about the collapse of communism.

'A work trip?' I had asked hopefully, when she suggested it. After I left the BBC staff and became freelance, my first assignment had been a trip to Israel and Cairo with Jenny as my producer.

'No. We'll have to pay our own way. Think of it as research. I've got lots of contacts. We *must* go. It's a historic time.'

Sunday 11th March

Budapest

Jenny's friend met us and drove us to an apartment in Bimbo Street where we are staying.

⌒

We were renting the apartment from friends of friends. It was comfortable, full of books and ornaments, with a small kitchen containing a rickety gas stove. The front door key was tricky, and so was the bath plug. Both had to be fiddled with in elaborate ways to make them work, but I had performed similar rituals in the house I grew up in. In certain domestic details, Eastern Europe in 1990 was not unlike Britain in the fifties. There was a loud, chiming clock in the living room that interrupted my sleep. On the third day I moved it further away, into the hall, and it fell silent. Fearing I had broken it, I moved it back again and it resumed its torturous hourly chime.

Hungary was preparing for elections. The communists had disbanded in October 1989 and a multitude of new parties had sprung up. Dutifully we attended a lecture given by Dr Géza Jeszenszky of the MDF (Hungarian Democratic Forum) about the various political parties: *decided we didn't support the MDF. The SDS (Alliance of Free Democrats) sounds the best bet*, I noted in my diary. Most of Jenny's Hungarian friends had reached the same conclusion. They were writers, mainly, and they were all currently translating the bestselling

American novel *The Hunt for Red October* by Tom Clancy, into Hungarian. A publisher wanted it done fast, to coincide with the release of the Sean Connery film version, so he had divided it up and distributed it chapter by chapter among the English-speaking literati of Budapest. On a couple of occasions puzzled intellectuals asked for help with nautical words. We were not much use.

All writers talk a lot about money; Hungarian writers seemed to do it even more than most. For many of them the collapse of Communism meant the end of their income.

Monday 12th March

We attended a meeting of Hungarian PEN. My old friend was there, and a lot of distinguished writers, publishers and filmmakers, all of whom seemed more concerned about the withdrawal of state subsidies than elated about the new democracy.

The 'old friend' was actually a former lover. He and I had a brief affair in Salzburg in 1976, when we both attended a seminar on American literature run by an organisation whose purpose might have been to flaunt Western luxuries and liberties to Eastern Europeans. The BBC sent several delegates each year.

The seminar was held in Schloss Leopoldskron, formerly the palatial lakeside home of theatre director Max Reinhardt. In the sixties, the schloss and its grounds had been used as the setting for the film *The Sound of Music*. The seminar leaders were writers and academics, mostly American; many of the participants were academics too, from all over Europe, with a large contingent from the East: Poland, Yugoslavia, Romania and Hungary. We discussed literature all day and drank in the *bierkeller* in the evenings. Not surprisingly, some of us felt cross-cultural attractions. There was a major obstacle, probably devised by the organisers of the seminar to prevent such romances blossoming: no one had their own bedroom. The majority of participants slept in dormitories of eight to ten people; I was among the more fortunate and shared a room with only two other women, a mad Swede whose alarm clock rang at seven every morning (unless I managed to press the stop button under cover of darkness the night before) and a neurotic Italian who lit her first cigarette soon after the Swede's alarm went off. It was not a place for dalliance.

It should have been possible to linger in the leafy and romantic grounds which surrounded the schloss, but this July had been particularly wet and everywhere was so muddy that open-air lovemaking was out of the question. We wandered disconsolately by the lakeside one Saturday night, comparing the merits of communism and democracy but thinking about other problems. He steered me towards a small summerhouse or gazebo. It was made of panes of glass but since it was night this didn't matter. At least the ground inside was dry, though very hard. There were a couple of stone benches. It wasn't comfortable. (Several years later, at Christmas, surrounded by family, watching *The Sound of Music* on television, I recognised that gazebo in the scene where the young Nazi woos the eldest von Trapp daughter and they sing a foolish song about being sixteen, going on seventeen.)

My love affair was not without pain (quite apart from the pressure of the concrete floor). He was unhappily married, he said; he was certainly unhappy. I was not unhappily married, though I sometimes felt lonely. This affair was a defence against that loneliness. It couldn't do damage, I told myself. We parted at the end of the seminar with ambivalent feelings and I missed him.

'I know what happened in Salzburg,' said Paul, one evening, sitting in the living room after the children had gone to bed.

'What do you mean?' My heart did a little jump. Paul was frightening when he was jealous. His own susceptibilities did not make him tolerant of mine. I had been punished severely for my one previous lapse.

'The Hungarian. You had an affair.'

I didn't know what to say.

'How do you know?'

Paul prevaricated, then he told me he had received an anonymous letter from another participant at the seminar.

I was horrified and ashamed. Puzzled too. Speculating about the identity of the letter writer obsessed me. Was it the Italian or the Swede? They may have been aware of me creeping into the bedroom late at night. It could have been anyone, though I thought I'd been discreet. Perhaps everyone had been discussing me with disapproval. In some ways I disapproved myself. This wasn't like my first affair, which had been a mixture of getting my own back and trying to find out what the rules were in our marriage. (Some people in those days not only practised open marriage but advocated it on idealistic grounds.) One rule was absolutely clear by now: my having sex with other men was unacceptable. And I had known that.

I apologised to Paul, who was surprisingly easily mollified and I lived with my guilt until it dwindled to the point at which I could smile at the memory of what, in a certain mood, seemed harmless enough. Twice I had strayed; twice I had been caught. I wasn't very good at infidelity; I would give it up. My resolve lasted some time, but not forever.

Many, many years later, Paul admitted that there had been no anonymous letter, just a note from me to the Hungarian which he had found in my handbag before I posted it. The letter had been affectionate rather than passionate, making clear that I was happily married and had every intention of staying that way. This partly explained the low level of Paul's anger. Another part of the explanation was that he had also been having a love affair while I was away, with a woman who later married another famous author.

The Hungarian and I had exchanged a couple of letters, then dropped all contact until this chance meeting, fourteen years later, at PEN. In the meantime, he told me, he had divorced and remarried. Would Jenny and I like to come to tea tomorrow?

He lived just outside the city in a light, prettily furnished house with a garden. His young wife was a librarian. He had courted her while changing his books. She didn't speak English, but smiled a lot and brought us tea and cakes while we had an earnest conversation about writers in Hungary.

'I am not in favour of these state subsidies,' he said in his precise English. 'It is good they are ending. There are too many obscure poets living on handouts. Now they must take up a more useful occupation.'

I asked him what he was writing at the moment.

'A novel. But it is a novel based on real characters. Do you know Otto Weininger?'

I confessed my knowledge of him was limited.

He explained who he was and how he figured in the book. He said Franz Kafka, Georg Lukács and Sigmund Freud were also characters in it.

'I can't quite see it rivalling *The Hunt for Red October*,' commented Jenny, as we sat on the bus back to town.

'At least he seems a happy man now. I'm glad.'

Later that week a mutual friend in Budapest told us that my friend's divorce from his first wife had been what you might call acrimonious. At one point he had chased her round the garden with an axe.

Otto Weininger, I discovered, was a raving anti-Semite and misogynist who wrote one book and killed himself when he was 23.

Monday 19th March

Left Budapest early and flew to Prague where we booked into the Europa Hotel on Wenceslas Square. The hotel is a fabulous art nouveau building with a winding staircase and rooms built in ascending circles. My bedroom, for which I pay 510 krona a night (£10 at the tourist rate of exchange) has double wooden doors, carved panels (on the wardrobe doors bunches of fruit hang from bows), a chandelier – and a very hard bed.

⌒

The Czechs had forced the communists to resign in November 1989. On 29th December, Václav Havel had been sworn in as President and Alexander Dubček, hero and victim of the events of '68 which led to the Soviet invasion, was elected chairman of the Federal Assembly in Prague.

People in Prague seemed more optimistic about their democratic future than the Hungarians had been. It wasn't paradise and never would be: shop assistants were surly as though having to sell their wares was a form of exploitation; government offices were both chaotic and bureaucratic. But the Czechs were proud of their Velvet Revolution. They had created a legend. They had put flowers in the muzzles of rifles. They had rung bells to signal a new era. Those who had been in prison had been set free and rewarded with high office. Some of them had been brave.

A friend of Jenny's, Helena Klíma, met us for lunch; once she had worked in publishing, now she was a psychotherapist. She and her husband, the writer Ivan Klíma, had been active in the Charter 77 movement and because of that their daughter had been refused a place at university. Talking about those who left the country during the hard years and those who stayed, I said it was braver to stay. She demurred.

'Going or staying can be brave. Or cowardly. It depends.'

Journalists and broadcasters were eager to talk and pass on ideas for stories, which I jotted down: *the gypsies; the environmental damage caused by Soviet troops; the re-emergence of religious life (monks and nuns coming out of hiding)*. A heavy-metal rock group who had recorded protest songs turned up at the hotel to be interviewed. Their English was poor, but later I made a short radio feature using tiny snippets of what they said, illustrating their comments with noisy music from a cassette they pressed on us.

We also did what all tourists do in Prague, waited in the Old Town Centre for the clock to reach the hour and the twelve apostles to appear in jerky procession at the top of the tower. In fact we did this several times, enjoying most of all the occasion on which the hour came and nothing happened. No apostles processed; no bird flapped its wings, no chimes sounded. Tourist cameras were lowered disconsolately. It was the day after the change to summer time and the attempt to advance the clock had disrupted the mechanism. We walked over the Charles Bridge and explored St Vitus Cathedral and Prague Castle, looking for the window from which three Catholic representatives of the Habsburg Emperor had been thrown by Bohemians in 1618, provoking the Thirty Years' War. Presumably, if there had been no defenestration in Prague, something else would have plunged Europe into bloody conflict between Protestants and Catholics, destined to be mortal enemies for far longer than communists and capitalists.

There was a big red octopus slumped in Wenceslas Square with a placard saying it represented Soviet domination. It seemed to be made of rubber.

Friday 23rd March

Two bank clerks arrived at the hotel and said they had mistaken my dollar traveller's cheques for pounds and asked for the difference back! I gave it and they were incredibly relieved and grateful.

I had the impression they would have been punished severely for their mistake, perhaps made to pay back the money out of their own pockets. But such things happen in both communist and capitalist societies: people without power pay dearly for their lapses.

Sunday 25th March

We flew back to London arriving home at 5pm.

Louis is here.

⌐

My son's presence made being home easier. Much of the time he stayed in his room, headphones clamped to his ears, studying while listening to music. The pulsating of the heavy rhythms gave life to the house. In the evenings we ate together before he went out with his friends. Preparing the familiar food I knew he liked (especially fish parcels, kedgeree, poached eggs and baked beans on toast) was a comforting link with the past.

'Tell me more about Prague and Budapest.' We sat opposite each other at one end of the long, pine, family table. I told him about the clocks, the bath plugs, the bank clerks, the political parties, the gypsies, the pop group and the window they chucked the blokes from in the 17th century.

'I'm thinking of visiting Eastern Europe in the summer,' he said, gathering up the used plates. 'There are work camps there for students.' He took the plates into the kitchen, then stuck his head back round the door. 'I must go. I'm meeting Joe and Adam.' He fetched his bike from the shed. The garden gate opened and closed and I imagined him cycling through dark streets in the rain. There was no point staying awake till he returned. Experience suggested that in the morning the door of his room would be shut and he would be safely sleeping inside.

Later I spoke to Marcel on the phone.

'Mum! How are you doing?'

'I've just got back from Prague.'

'Tell me about it.'

I made my account brief, because I sensed he had something to tell me. He said he had been asked by a publisher to collect material for a guide to the Soviet Union and was planning to set out in June or July.

'That's great! But I wonder if it will still be there.' I described the defeated red octopus in Wenceslas Square.

'Of course it will still be there,' he said. 'But it will be different. That's what's interesting.'

Perhaps the same could be said of our family. Still there, but different. No longer sitting together at the table but still in touch, still part of each other's lives. Except that Paul and I hadn't spoken since he left. We had agreed it would be better that way; a few months' silence. But he was due to come to London soon, for the publication of his latest book.

I dreaded his visit and longed for it.

Chapter 6

April

Monday 2nd April

Went to St George's for blood test.

Tuesday 3rd April

Paul arrived in England.

⌒

April threatened to be a cruel month.

I had an AIDS test at the local hospital, giving a false name – Jackson – and then forgetting to respond when it was called. The test was negative and I don't think I ever seriously feared a different result. It could have been worse, but going to the hospital, sitting in the waiting room, talking to the sympathetic young counsellor, I had to struggle with feelings of shame. I told myself that I was being responsible and preparing to start a new life, perhaps abroad.

'Why do you think you might be HIV positive?'

'Well, my husband's been having an affair with someone from California and that's a pretty high-risk area. My ex-husband, perhaps I should say. We've separated.'

'With a woman or a man?'

'Oh, a woman.' I felt wrong-footed because it hadn't occurred to me that the counsellor would think my husband's lover might be a man. Was that my prejudice? 'My husband was unfaithful with a woman. Quite a few women, actually, over the years. I don't know exactly how many. That's still risky, isn't it?'

'Yes. There is a risk and it's responsible of you to have a check-up, Mrs Jackson.'

Thank you very much. When I went back a few days later and heard that the test was negative, he said he wasn't going to give me the usual advice about taking precautions in future. I wasn't sure whether to be pleased or offended. Was I too respectable or too old?

Paul returned to London – not to see me but to launch his new book, *Chicago Loop*, a dark fantasy from some chamber of his mind to which I didn't have the key. There was a party to celebrate the publication and I was sent an invitation by the publisher on which I scrawled a rude refusal before putting it in a drawer, where many years later Paul found it, at a time when the message and the anger were no longer relevant. My diary shows a series of cancelled invitations: 'Should have gone to dinner with X but couldn't face it'; 'Arranged to meet Y for drinks, then rang to make excuses.'

Tuesday 10th April

VSO have no job for me. I want to die.

⌒

It was one of those bland official letters which, torn open at the wrong moment in your life, thrust personal insult and rejection in your face, rubbing it in as you re-read. It said there were no jobs available at the moment in my area of expertise (broadcasting). The dream of sunshine, worthwhile work, new friends, a new love – shimmered like a mirage about to dissolve and behind it was a darker picture in which a woman of a certain age, whose children had left home and whose husband no longer wanted her, shuffled through rainy streets alone, muttering to herself. Was this what I was choosing?

I had refused to see Paul and spoiled the invitation to his party. When he came to the house to visit Louis, I went out. A six-month separation was what we agreed, I thought; only three months had passed. He was in London on a promotional trip, a coincidence which changed nothing. No words that could make a difference had been said.

Then I weakened.

Saturday 14th April (Easter Eve)

My parents came for lunch. Louis and Susanna were here too. Then in the evening when they had left, Paul came over and stayed the night.

Sunday 15th April (Easter Day)

Went for a walk with Paul to Polesden Lacey. We talked and got on well.

On that walk across the hills of Surrey and through the grounds of the stately home we had visited many times with the children, the trees in new leaf and the daffodils blooming, we quoted Chaucer: *Whan that Aprill with his shoures soote, the droghte of March hath perced to the roote…* – a single sentence describing Spring which we could both recite, or thought we could, in the original Middle English, culminating in, *thanne longen folk to goon on pilgrimages.* * Paul talked confidently of resuming our life together one day, though the words 'but not yet' hovered unspoken. We were planning different pilgrimages. At the end of that sunny day Paul left again, to fly back to America; I stayed in Wandsworth feeling slightly better. A night and a day with him had revived me.

VSO had no job at present – but that didn't mean they would never have one. My postings officer said she was 'hawking my CV around'. Assuming that eventually someone in some warm corner of the world would want me, I bought two summer dresses and began a course of inoculations.

Friday 20th April

Set out for Crouch End and my VSO post-selection course at a TUC conference centre. Food is quite good. The people seem OK. Met a farmer, who is going to Mongolia, leaving his wife behind – perhaps it isn't such an odd thing to do.

⌣

The thought had nagged me from time to time that if I were sent far away and if Paul and I decided to stay married, we might face a situation like our argumentative courtship, when I wanted to stay in Africa and he wanted to leave. Yet here was a man, about my age or even a little older, whose wife was prepared to wait for two years while he went to Mongolia. Or you could look at it another way: here was a man who had been posted to Mongolia and whose wife was unwilling to go with him.

---

* The opening of the prologue to *The Canterbury Tales* by Chaucer.

'Someone's got to keep an eye on the farm,' he explained. 'My son will do the hard work, but my wife is good with the accounts. Also, she doesn't want to leave the grandchildren. The little one is only six months.'

'Will she visit you?'

'Oh yes. At least once. I'll take time off. Show her the sights of Ulan Bator.'

The arrangement could be a sign of the strength of their marriage or of their mutual indifference; perhaps not even they knew which.

Paul and I had spent a lot of time apart. I usually said I didn't mind, but that wasn't always true. It was hard when he left and I became a single parent; it was hard when he came back. In 1973 he returned after four months on *The Great Railway Bazaar* trip to learn that I had been unfaithful; I gave loneliness as my excuse.

'What about women whose husbands are in prison?' he demanded, raging.

'It's not the same,' I attempted, defiant but fearful.

'Or fighting in wars? Or exploring? What about Penelope?'

Was waiting faithfully the right way? It sometimes seemed a waste of time, like Penelope's weaving. Was it admirable to remain chaste when Ulysses was in the arms of Circe?

On one occasion our roles were reversed: in 1984 Paul waited for me, for three months while I travelled in southern Africa, researching the role of women in Lesotho, Botswana and Swaziland, three countries which provided migrant workers for the South African mines. In Lesotho I went into villages consisting entirely of women; they farmed the poor soil and sold vegetables in the market in order to feed, clothe and educate their children, struggling to get by until the end of the month when the lucky ones would receive money from their absent husbands. Because they were women, they couldn't get credit from the bank.

At the end of the three months, Paul and the boys had met me in Nairobi and we revisited some of the places we had last seen in the sixties, including Embu Girls School and a hotel in the White Highlands where Paul and I had spent the night on our journey from Embu to Kampala to get married. It had been a smart hotel in those days; by 1984 it was dusty and dilapidated, and we were the only guests. But on that holiday we also went to wonderful places we had never visited before – a bird sanctuary by a lake and a game reserve – and the future had seemed full of hope.

Saturday 21st April

The day was spent mainly discussing cultural attitudes — we had to choose people to take to a desert island from a list including 'gay nurse', 'Nigerian doctor' etc. Most people tried to be very 'right on'. Then we had to list discriminated groups, discuss images of the Third World, watch a video called 'Being White'.

The introductory course in 1990 was very different from the one I went on in 1965; then, in a special 'girls only' session, we had been advised by an American woman to take a year's supply of sanitary towels if we were going to a rural area, and not to date African men. I had ignored her advice.

Sunday 22nd April

The course ended soon after lunch and I came home feeling hopeful and refreshed.

~

One way or another I had a future, I assured myself. It might be abroad, it might be with Paul. Meanwhile I was making some programmes about Thomas Hardy, my favourite novelist, recording in West Dorset, at various places associated with Hardy: the cottage where he was born, the house called Max Gate which he designed, the replica of his study in the Dorchester museum, the churchyard at Stinsford where he was buried.

All these sites are near the village where Paul, Marcel, Louis and I had spent the winter of 1972, having come to England from Singapore, spoilt by sunshine and servants, to face cold weather, poverty and power cuts. Paul had written most of his Singapore novel, *Saint Jack*, there and our five months in Dorset inspired *The Black House*, about an academic and his wife who return from abroad to live in rural England.

Even after we moved to London, we continued to visit Dorset often, because my parents lived there for fifteen years after my father's retirement. (That was why we had rented a cottage there in 1972.) Then they moved to Sussex and our links with Dorset were broken. I was glad of the opportunity to return.

One programme was about Hardy's life. Another was about the novels and for this Furze Swann, a tour guide of Hardy country, took my producer, Joy Boatman, and myself to places which are important in the books: the church where Jude worked as a stonemason, the amphitheatre outside Dorchester where Henchard meets the wife he sold twenty years earlier in *The Mayor of Casterbridge*, the house where Bathsheba lived in *Far From the Madding Crowd*, the Vale of the Great Dairies, where Tess met Angel Clare.

And I interviewed Tess of the d'Urbervilles herself. Anyone who has seen a photograph of the young Gertrude Bugler, who played the doomed country girl in a local, dramatised version produced with Hardy's co-operation, will know that she embodied Tess, with her thick dark hair, innocent eyes and smooth cheeks.

Tuesday 24th April

We drove to Beaminster and talked to Gertrude Bugler who at 92 still has a beautiful face and remembers the days when she played Tess, and Hardy came to rehearsals, and how Florence Hardy asked her not to go to London to be in the West End production of the play, because Hardy would go to her dressing room and his reputation would be damaged.

Most people say Hardy was in love with her, but she says (and believes) it was a totally innocent relationship.

Hardy's first wife, Emma, seems to have degenerated during the span of their marriage from soulmate to 'nagging shrew', ignored and neglected by her husband when he formed an attachment to Florence Dugdale, who became the second Mrs Hardy soon after Emma's death. Hearing and reading their story again, I felt sorry for Emma and decided Thomas Hardy had treated her shabbily.

After Emma died and Hardy married Florence, he missed his first wife desperately and wrote love poems to her, making Florence jealous. He repeated his neglectful behaviour and the infidelities in his second marriage; he did fall in love with Gertrude Bugler, suggesting at one point that she should elope with him. She was too innocent or perhaps too wise to take his advances seriously.

April 30th 1990

Dear Paul,

I recently returned from Wessex where I interviewed Gertrude Bugler in Beaminster (the old lady who played Tess and Hardy fell in love with) and various other Hardy buffs in the Dorchester area. It was very enjoyable and a bit nostalgic to see the place where I used to take Marcel to play group and the countryside where we were so miserable all those years ago!

(Funnily enough while I was there I had the feeling we had been rather happy in Dorset, but you have told me so many times what a pain I was that I suppose that must be the truth of it and the happy memories are just an illusion.)

I decided there are many points of comparison between T. Hardy and P. Theroux. Consider the following facts about T.H.

1) Brilliant novelist.

2) Artistic tendencies – i.e. could draw a bit.

3) Humble origins and determination to rise.

4) Became very wealthy as a result of writing novels.

5) Despite this, 'careful' with money.

6) Built own house as mark of success.

7) *Became highly sought after especially by literary ladies who wanted to tell him he was wonderful and were turned on by his sexy books.*

8) *Liked being told he was wonderful by aforesaid ladies and sometimes fell in love with them.*

9) *Workaholic, ignoring everyone around him.*

10) *Fell in love with and married lively outgoing woman, slightly above him on the social scale.*

11) *Wife helped him with writing, went walking and cycling with him, helped him in his rise to fame but found it hard to fit into his life.*

12) *Started to neglect wife and pay attention to other women.*

13) *Wrote a book his wife hated (*Jude the Obscure*).*

How's that for starters?

Paul's only quibble with my jaunty note was about our relative social standing. Did I really think I came from above him on the social scale? It wasn't a point I would insist on. Our unpretentious origins were a bond between us. So was the subliminal message we had both been slipped by our parents at the beginning of our lives: *you can do better than we have done.* It was a demanding piece of programming, all the harder to live with because at times our parents seemed to have forgotten their instructions and resented us carrying them out. Our birthplaces were separated by thousands of miles, but we had both grown up and learned to rebel in similar living rooms, clean and neat with copies of *The Reader's Digest* on the coffee table and knick-knacks on the mantelpiece. We tried to leave those homes behind, going first to university and then to Africa, and then marrying an outsider (though our exogamy was cautious: we dated Africans but didn't have children with them).

I wonder now, looking back, if Paul had imagined when he met me that I was an upper-middle-class English girl whose parents had a big house in the country with a library and an art collection; if so he hid his disappointment well when we arrived, jet-lagged, at the semi in SW16, a few days after our Kampala wedding. As for me, I was delighted by the big, noisy family in Medford, Massachusetts who welcomed me enthusiastically a fortnight later, at the end of 1967. Though the living room might look similar, the atmosphere in his family's house was very different, with five boys aged from twelve to 28 competing for attention and two girls and two parents looking on and applauding. In my family there were only two girls and two parents. My older brother had died at birth; I had taken his place. I was used to a good deal of applause myself.

Perhaps I did deceive Paul when we first met, not about my social standing, but about my character. In *My Secret History* Andre Parent reflects: '*I had married a pretty girl but she had quickly become a discontented woman.*' On our early dates in Kampala and for much of our brief courtship, I appeared not only pretty, but smiling and compliant: inside I was anxious and ambitious, though I wasn't sure what I wanted to do with my life. I tried to explain this, and he nodded and smiled and nibbled my ear. He knew exactly what he wanted to do: his first novel, *Waldo*, was about to be published; he was a writer. He wanted encouragement, affection, family life and for me to want what he wanted. In his family, boys competed and achieved; girls supported and applauded. He thought I would be like his sisters; instead I was more like his brothers, questioning, mocking and wanting my share of recognition. I disappointed him, and I felt disappointed because he didn't value what I most valued in myself.

While researching the Hardy programmes, I listened to a recording of the poem which begins:

Woman much missed, how you call to me, call to me,
Saying that now you are not as you were
When you had changed from the one who was all to me,
But as at first, when our day was fair. *

It made me cry.

'Sometimes I feel you love me best when I'm far away,' I told Paul. When he travelled, and even now that we were estranged, his letters were always loving; when we lived together, I became the grumpy and dissatisfied Emma Hardy.

On the last day of April I met a friend for dinner. She had been married for a long time to a well-known writer; he had left her, wounding her severely, three years earlier. Over dinner she told me that on a recent walking holiday in Malta, she had started an ardent affair. *She is transformed. All her hurt and sadness gone away. God, I wish it would happen to me.*

* 'The Voice' by Thomas Hardy, 1914.

Chapter 7

May

Thursday 3rd May

Drove to Hatfield to interview Barbara Cartland.

⌒

I was preparing for a walking holiday in Crete, hoping I might meet a man who would rescue me from sadness and despair, so this was a timely interview for *Ex Libris* (aka *Writers' Bookshelves*) with the most popular writer of romantic fiction in the world.

She lives in a huge Victorian house with lovely grounds and a large staff. She's nearly 89, wore pink, lots of make-up including false eyelashes and hair bouffing out around her head (from the back she's a bit bald on the crown). It was hard getting her to talk about the books in her library – she wanted to talk about her own books and her views on sex, love, gypsies, the poll tax …

⌒

'Do you know, I've just finished my 513th book. I heard today that I'm the favourite writer of … oh, what's his name? You know, the naughty one …' She said something that sounded like Godolphin. 'You know who I mean. In the Middle East.'

'Not Colonel Gaddafi?'

'Yes, yes. He loves my novels. So did Anwar Sadat. I used to give his wife copies of my books and he would take them away from her to read first. But everyone likes them. Last summer, when it was very hot, a firm of butchers offered a free copy of one of my books with every £12 worth of meat he sold. Do you know how many he gave away? Three-hundred-thousand!'

'Why do so many people like your books?'

'It's the message.'

'What message?'

'The importance of beauty and love.'

I could find no fault with that. 'But of course, you don't believe in sex before marriage.'

'No, I don't and I'll tell you why. I've been all around the world and I've never met a man of any colour, creed, class or nationality who wants to go into a room with the woman who is his wife and the mother of his children and wonder how many other men have been to bed with her,' she said. 'I say to the young girls now, who don't listen needless to say, I say it's a man's job to want to go to bed with you. He says please, please, please. It's your job to say no, and I'll tell you why. If you give in, he says that's wonderful, marvellous, but at the back of his mind he really despises you. The great thing is to say no, no, no until you're married. Sex before marriage is wrong. And it's the woman who is hurt, not the man. Men can be very sentimental; they produce the best love poems like Byron, the best love paintings like Botticelli, the best music like Chopin; no woman can rival them when it comes to sentimentality about love. But a man can have a love affair and it can mean no more than having a good meal; it can be entirely a physical act; for a woman it is always an emotional experience.'

Yes, men are like that, I thought, surprised by a frisson of sympathy. The men in Barbara Cartland's novels, under their foppish clothes, resembled Elisabeth Frink's heroes and thugs.

When I asked if the heroines in her books always lived happily once they were married, her answer was less certain than I had expected.

'I hope they do. People want them to. I hope they will, because if you look for the real love ... the real love is when you find the other half of yourself. The Greeks believed that God made one person and he said I'm lonely, so God cut him in half and one half was the woman and she was the spiritual side, the soft side, the gentle side, the lover of children and he was the strong man, the protector, the fighter, keeping her for his special use and together they made one person; and that's what you look for. The Greeks believed that when you come into this world you look for the other half of yourself.'

I disagreed with most of what she said – but I couldn't help quite liking her. We had tea and she presented me with a copy of one of her books, signed and gift wrapped.

I certainly felt I had lost half of myself when Paul left and I didn't know how to stop the pain. There was a lot going for me: I was working hard at my radio programmes, getting support from my women friends, spending time with my family and enjoying the company of occasional visitors: Louis and his girlfriend, Susanna, were often at the house; a friend of theirs whose boyfriend had beaten her up took refuge for a few nights; a disc jockey from Zimbabwe joined us one Sunday for lunch and a game of frisbee on the common. There were many pleasures in my life, yet it was not a whole life.

I need a cause, I thought and attended an introductory meeting at The Samaritans, imagining myself waiting by a telephone to rescue desperate people for whom life had lost its meaning (I see now that I myself needed rescuing). I learned to my surprise that if someone really wants to die, the Samaritans don't rush to the house to prevent the suicide; the final choice lies with the individual.

I joined a charity which helps the poor and spent an uncomfortable weekend at a dilapidated house in the country, scraping and sanding interior walls to make a holiday home for disadvantaged London families. Again, the impulse to help those in need sprang from my own needs: without Paul, I felt seriously disadvantaged. I knew I was well-off in many important ways; I had a house, money, work and opportunities for travel. But my own emotional needs remained unmet. Hope for the future was elusive. The nagging pain was still there, a constant dull ache which tired me out, so that at the end of the day I felt I deserved the relief of a strong drink, or a joint.

The two drugs were very different. Alcohol had a predictable, enlivening effect and I could monitor how it was affecting me very clearly. It was a sociable drug and I enjoyed drinking with friends. Marijuana, on the other hand, was a solitary and intense pleasure. I knew that once I had smoked the weed I would be fit for nothing other than lying in bed with my head spinning and floating among the outer planets of the universe, far away from the pains and pleasures of the earth.

If love was too much to hope for, sex might offer a similar escape. We had separated, so it was no longer forbidden. But who could I have it with? I ran through possible candidates in my mind and in my address book, summoning up former lovers and friends who might possibly become lovers, turning them over in my memory and occasionally making a phone call that led to a date. Because nostalgia played its usual tricks, I remembered only the good things about each of these past relationships and then when the man and I were looking at each other across a restaurant table, committed to a whole evening together, I would be reminded (like the character in a Katherine Mansfield story called 'A Dill Pickle'*) of why it had ended, or never been consummated. One man had been, very briefly, a lover at Oxford. On our last evening together in 1964 in his college room, he had drunk too much and been sick; when we met up again more than 25 years later, he started nervously glugging first beer and then wine and after one course of an Italian meal hurriedly left the table. He returned with the relieved but shaken look of someone whose antipasto has hit the porcelain. Another old friend, characterised even in his twenties by a no-bullshit approach to life which was refreshing but not romantic, now talked too forthrightly over a meal I paid for, about the practical advantages of being with a woman of independent means; another simply talked too much so that by the end of the evening I was exhausted.

The only person I actually had sex with during these months, and then not very often, was an old friend and occasional lover.

We had met in the early eighties and worked together on several programmes. Together we went to interview Yehudi Menuhin, discussed a film set in Martinique and a landmark production of *Guys and Dolls* at the National Theatre. It was exciting work. He was an attractive man. Eventually he propositioned me with words that made my heart beat as fast as that of a Barbara Cartland heroine.

'I really fancy you,' he said.

Scared, I backed off. I hadn't had an affair since the Hungarian in Salzburg five or six years earlier and I had

* 'A Dill Pickle', *Bliss and Other Stories* by Katherine Mansfield, 1920.

promised myself I wouldn't. I sent him a postcard saying 'I fancy you too, but I don't think it would be a good idea to do anything about it.' 'Yet' was written in invisible ink at the end of that sentence, which was carefully worded to leave all possibilities open.

A few months later, I found out about Paul and the English teacher in Pennsylvania. It wasn't the sex that I minded; it was the declarations of love, the discussions as to what to do about 'your wife' and the revelation that this had been going on for more than a year. (No wonder I had felt lonely and in need of love myself.) We had a tearful confrontation, he went to America, partly at my insistence ('Go on, go then. Spend time with her if that's what you want. I'll manage without you.') and I stayed in London, wounded and frightened – a rehearsal for the present.

I had rung my friend one day from work and suggested we met for a drink. 'I'll come over to your place if you like.'

'That would be very nice.'

The affair made me feel better. It restored some of the pride and pleasure that had been shattered by my husband's preference for another woman. It was enjoyable without making heavy emotional demands. Occasionally there was a hint it might become more; we liked each other – could this feeling tip into love? We didn't let it.

Now, some years later, I was still able to ring him and arrange to meet. We would make love and then go our separate ways for a month or so until the danger of real intimacy had passed.

Around this time, in May 1990, because I was lonely and fond of him, I vaguely thought we might live together, not as lovers but as friends. I needed someone to keep me company while Louis was away at Oxford; he needed somewhere to live. This thought was in his mind too, I was sure. 'Let's meet for lunch next week,' he suggested on the phone, the day after we had spent an evening together. 'There's something I want to discuss with you.' But true to form, he postponed the lunch and then postponed it again and eventually I gave up the idea of making this relationship more substantial.

My friend later became a successful crime writer and recently I recognised myself in one of his characters. The woman, fair-haired with floating clothes and trendy specs, is a former lover of the detective (a tough-talking version of the author) and the wife of a successful television director. In the story, they meet again and resume their affair – until the detective discovers the woman is responsible for the murder he is investigating: she has killed her husband's girlfriend. I glimpsed beneath the rather torrid story the faint palimpsest of real events.

Friday 18th May

I'm at Gatwick waiting for my flight to Athens.

My purse was stolen at Clapham Junction between ten to six and five to six, after buying my ticket. The plane has been delayed.

Saturday 19th May

Arrived in Athens at about six in the morning and went to a hotel in the centre. I have to share a room with a woman called Kay.

~

I had booked to go on a group walking holiday. This was an unpromising start. First the lost purse which contained cash and keys. Then the long wait at the airport and the early morning arrival, feeling unwell. (The days when I could sit on the floor of the night train to Florence and step out ready to confront great art were long gone.) Then, worst of all, the discovery that I had to share a room. I didn't want to sleep near another human being. I wanted to crawl into my own lair.

'The lady you are sharing with arrived yesterday,' said the tour guide, handing me a key.

A tall, sun-tanned woman stepped out of the shower, wrapped in a towel, her hair covered in purple foam. She shook my hand and said in an American accent, 'Hi, I'm Kay. As soon as my hair's done I'll take a walk and let you sleep for a couple of hours. Then maybe you'd like to visit the Acropolis with me?'

She didn't seem too bad, I thought, closing my eyes and trying to ignore the sun that infiltrated the shuttered windows. Could have been worse.

Could have been a lot worse. Kay was a bit like me – similar age, tall, slim and fair, with blue eyes. She came from Boise, Idaho where she worked as a buyer in a store. I guessed that at one time she had been a model – she took care of her appearance in a professional, unfussy way, never used a handbag but wore a pouch strapped to her waist and a small leather rucksack slung over one shoulder. She turned out to be the best walker in the group, skipping ahead up rocky paths, brown legs in white trainers, while the rest of us plodded behind, in our walking boots and thick socks. She liked gadgets and gear, had special non-rustling bags for packing her clothes inside her rucksack and an implement for heating water in a cup which she used to make us both coffee every morning. My short-wave radio intrigued her, though at first she mocked my evening dance around the room as I tried to coax intelligible sounds from it.

'It's just squeaking and whistling.'

'But listen,' I said. 'It's the news.'

And sure enough, the measured voice of a World Service news reader verified what we knew only too well: that there was a heatwave in Athens.

'That's great! Where can I get one?'

Kay appears in more than half the photos I took on that holiday, peering into pots on ancient sites, striding along clifftop paths, just as I appear in hers (I know because she sent me copies). We became close, as people who share a room and like each other do, but we never saw each other again after the holiday ended and only wrote once each.

Set out to Piraeus and took the overnight ferry to Crete. I shared a cabin with Kay, Rachel and Joy. I felt very ill – I have been suffering from cystitis – and vomited.

⌒

The other two who shared the cabin on the ferry, Rachel and Joy, appear in fewer pictures and stir up fewer memories. Rachel was a middle-aged American who had a tendency to drink too much; one night she barged into the wrong hotel and fell asleep in the foyer. Joy was a plump Australian who wore tight cycling shorts and took the walking very seriously, though she often lagged at the tail end of the group, out of breath and sweating. The dozen others in the party, dispersed in clusters to different cabins, included a family of five, a couple in their sixties who were always boasting or complaining, three or four young single women and two young single men. 'Not much chance of a man for us,' whispered Kay, who was divorced and had two sons, like me. The guide was a jolly young woman, who on one occasion was reduced to tears by the complainers. All these people appear in group pictures – round a table in a restaurant, scrambling out of a van to begin the next walk, filing along a narrow track in the gorge of Samaria.

Although I didn't know it as I crouched in the tiny loo on the ferry that first night, being sick and trying not to wake my companions, it was to be a good holiday. After a few days of sunshine and walking I felt better. There was no romantic hero in sight but my body and soul were restored. I was hungry again. I slept well each night and woke up ready for the day.

Wednesday 30th May

Went to Phaistos, the second-largest Minoan ruin. Kay and I each had a different guidebook and enjoyed figuring out what was what – the theatre, the grand staircase, the various magazines and royal apartments.

The ancient city of Phaistos has not been heavily restored and requires some effort to imagine its former glory. As we approached the site we met another member of the party – it was Rachel, the boozy American – returning after only five minutes. She looked disappointed.

'Is this it?' I asked, gesturing to the ruins ahead and wondering if we were on the right path.

'That's it, just this pile of old rocks,' she said. Kay used this as a caption on the photo of Phaistos she sent me: *just a pile of old rocks*. And the words echoed those of a guide touting for business in Athens. 'You do not need a guide to see the Acropolis,' he said. 'But without one, you will be looking at meaningless stones.'

Knossos was more spectacular. Kay and I visited it twice. On the first occasion there was a fire nearby, smoke billowed over the palace and we had to be evacuated. We were relieved to find it unharmed when we returned next day. Purists disapprove of the over-confident recreation of Minoan life and claim that it owes more to Sir Arthur Evans, the excavator, than to King Minos (of whom there were many). 'There is little doubt,' says one pursed-lipped authority, 'that in order to create an impression, Evans in many instances overstepped the mark and some restoration is mere conjecture.' Evans himself insisted that his restoration gave a true impression of the later palace – the one rebuilt in the second millennium BC – though he admitted that 'to the casual visitor ... the attempt may well at times seem overbold, and the lover of picturesque ruins may receive a shock.'* On the other hand, those who are disappointed by the pile of old rocks purporting to be Phaistos, will find Knossos more to their taste.

* These quotes came from a guidebook which I no longer own.

*Went to the archaeological museum where the stuff from Knossos
is displayed — the famous bull's head, the snake goddess, urns and
wonderful frescoes: the dolphins, the athletes with the bull, the
prince with lilies.*

You must have seen the picture of the athletes with the bull; it's
a favourite postcard. One figure is upside down, somersaulting
length-wise along the back of the prancing beast; another waits
at the rear end with arms outstretched to catch the vaulter and
a third stands in front, as if controlling the horns. The somersaulting figure is a boy, the other two are girls. The fresco has
been heavily restored and in an attempt at integrity, the restored
parts are a different colour and texture, to distinguish them
from the original fragments. The whole thing has been pieced
together centuries after it was first made, and extra bits added
where there were gaps. Did it look like that to the Cretan who
stepped back to admire the picture he had painted? And was
he proud to have portrayed the bull dance with such panache?

As a teenager, urged by the same forceful classics teacher
who persuaded me to boycott South African goods for 30 years,
I read Mary Renault's novel, *The King Must Die*, a retelling of
the legend of Theseus and the Minotaur which ties it to historical evidence about Minoan culture. My teacher said the fresco
of the bull vaulters must have inspired the novel. In the book,
Theseus volunteers to join the Athenian youths sent to Crete
as tribute to King Minos and becomes the leader of a team
of dancers who entertain the court by performing acrobatics
around a rampaging bull. Theseus' team becomes especially

proficient, practising their act with a mechanical bull made by the scientist Daedalus and they survive in the ring far longer than most dancers. Their enemies resort to doping the bull, making him mad and lethal and there's a final desperate fight in the bullring. Theseus kills the bull and escapes from Crete with his team of dancers and Ariadne, the King's daughter.

There are many more ingredients from the myth: the bestial lust of Queen Pasiphaë, the torment of King Minos, Theseus' journey through the labyrinth guided by Ariadne's thread, the betrayal on the island of Naxos when Ariadne becomes a follower of Dionysus. What is missing is the Minotaur himself, half-man half-bull, symbol of lust and death, a creature too strange to live in a book attempting realism.

Took a coach to the ferry – a grotty boat this time with no loo or shower in the cabin. It was quite rough but I slept like a log.

⌒

We spent a final day in Athens; it was a chance to revisit the Acropolis, with a guide to make sense of the meaningless stones, and to go round the museum which I had last visited in 1968. Paul and I had a 24-hour stopover in Athens on our way back to Uganda from London. Unfortunately there had been some sort of carnival going on, with people banging drums and blowing whistles, which kept us awake all night. Perhaps it was Mardi Gras. Paul said then and ever afterwards that he hated Greece. Now I had gone back without him, glad he was not there to complain.

Might my single status bring benefits?

Chapter 8

June

Saturday 2nd June

Left Athens at 4.30am and arrived at Gatwick at 6 our time.

Slept in the morning, got up lunchtime, shopped, unpacked and went to the Worgans' for dinner.

~

What kind of picture can I make from my scrappy diary entries during the weeks after my return from Crete? The fragments are not very promising. Substantial reconstruction will be needed. Some pieces may have to be discarded. Not the Worgans; my sister and her family. They are important; among the jottings in the diary for the month of June, their name appears at least half-a-dozen times, a recurring pattern in the muddle of my life.

Sunday 3rd June

Busy day – washing, sorting my things after the trip, over to the Worgans' to get hedge clippers, then home and gardening and a visit to the garden centre to get bedding plants and fertiliser. Was doing the garden when P.S. dropped by.

~

Should I have omitted the hedge clippers? I wasn't using them when he arrived. I was planting geraniums in the urns at the front of the house, hoping to make my pots as glorious as those clustered in Mediterranean courtyards. A car stopped, the front window was rolled down and a head with white hair and a rather red face looked out and shouted a greeting.

It was the man with whom I had an affair in 1973 when Paul was on *The Great Railway Bazaar* trip. In those days his hair wasn't white, his face wasn't red and I had been attracted to him for months. We were in daily contact at work. I had been married six years and had slept with no one other than Paul in that time. Paul had been unfaithful; he had confessed one affair and I had said it didn't matter. There had been others, unconfessed but suspected, and I told myself they didn't matter either. And if that was so, I reasoned disingenuously, why shouldn't I be unfaithful too? Anyway, you couldn't really call it 'being unfaithful' since it would make no difference to how I felt about my husband and children. Real love included granting freedom. But despite these rationalisations, the thought of being unfaithful, untrue, of breaking a promise I had intended to keep, shocked me.

Then Paul went away for four-and-a-half months to travel on the Orient Express and the Trans-Siberian Railway. I felt abandoned and angry, though I had grudgingly agreed he should go. At first my colleague and I arranged innocent daytime outings to museums and parks with the children. Then one evening I persuaded Inge, the Norwegian au pair, to babysit. We went to see a film called *The Conversation*, in which Gene Hackman is a surveillance expert, hired to spy on two lovers by the woman's wronged husband. Having recorded their conversation, he plays back one phrase over and over again. 'He'd kill us if he had the chance.' Hackman fears the man who hired him will murder the lovers. He becomes increasingly disturbed. But eventually it's the client who is found dead and when the tape is played once more, the emphasis is different. It has become 'He'd kill *us* if he had the chance': the lovers were justifying their plan to murder the husband. In one scene Gene Hackman flushes a toilet and blood bubbles up into the bowl.

At the time I made no conscious connection between the film and my situation. Desire, betrayal, jealousy and violence hovered in the night air as we walked through Covent Garden towards Charing Cross station and I ignored them, slipping my hand through my companion's arm. He stopped in his tracks, turned to face me and kissed me.

'I have loved you for so long, completely inadmissibly,' he said. Warmth flooded through me; not lust but a sudden balm.

We went home and slept together though we were too nervous to make love. Later, of course, we did. He became a family friend who occasionally stayed overnight. It wasn't the innocent affair it felt like; it did harm. Fifteen years later, in the chapter in *My Secret History* called 'Leaving Siberia', Paul gave the wife's lover the name Terry Slee and drew extensively on real events in his fictionalised account. The note found in the wife's handbag was real, word for word: *I would like to say in the nicest possible way that I love you in the nicest possible way.* The rage with the wife and the questioning of the children were real, alas. The attempt to humiliate Slee in front of his boss was real only up to a point: the culmination of that episode when Andre Parent (Paul's alter ego) holds up a dinner party and shoots the unfortunate lover in the eyes with a urine-filled water pistol did not take place.

We painstakingly pieced the marriage back together, but like a vase that has been broken and repaired, it was never the same again. My relationship with the lover became a friendship; we continued to meet from time to time but we had done too much damage to be very close. He was, for a while, on my list of men who might console me and we had been out to dinner once since Paul left. He told me he had recently married again

– his third attempt – and had two small children. His marriage was going through a bad patch but he was trying to make it work. I took him off my list. He had enough to worry about.

'What are you doing and why are you so brown?' he asked today.

'I'm planting geraniums. I've just come back from a walking holiday in Crete. Come in and have some tea.'

I prattled about the holiday. Silly stuff, to fill the void where passion had once been.

'It was the perfect combination: walking, swimming, history. I'm going to eat nothing but yoghurt and honey from now on. I had to share a room but she was a twin soul. Knossos caught fire while we were visiting but we went back the next day; you know, Sir Arthur Evans did the whole thing up the way he thought it should look, I don't think it's authentic; I got vertigo on one of the walks and couldn't look at the view.'

Prattling can be fun. The saddest thing about living alone is having no one to talk to each day; given the chance at last, impressions of Crete came tumbling out like snaps just back from the developer, unsifted and too numerous.

I waved goodbye feeling happy. I didn't see him again; perhaps my holiday memories were too tedious; more likely he was preoccupied with his own problems.

Paul has said the break-up of our marriage in 1989 was rooted in this affair of 1973, that he never got over the pain, jealousy and humiliation. That may be true. Perhaps the affair indicated a dangerous flaw in our relationship, a weakness in the marital bedrocks of loyalty and commitment. Or perhaps it was my way of screaming, 'This is what it feels like. Is this what you really want?'

Monday 4th June

Made phone calls and paid bills then walked across Wandsworth Common, down Trinity Road and across Tooting Bec Common to ascertain water temperature at the swimming pool. (64°)

~

Tooting Bec Lido (formerly Tooting Bec Baths) is the biggest swimming pool in Britain – a hundred yards long. It was built at the turn of the century. My grandfather swam in it and so did my father, who said he used to break the ice in winter; he taught me to swim there. Later I went with my friend Louise throughout the summer. In my early teens I swam a mile – eighteen lengths. It wasn't tiring, just boring and my fingers went numb and crinkly. By the following year I was fifteen and had changed from a child to a woman. Other things had become more important than swimming long distances; besides, it ruined your hairstyle. The pool became the place where Louise and I stalked romance. Over a two-month period I fell in love at least three times – with a lifeguard named Roy who was a student at a northern university (this relationship was limited to philosophical conversations at the poolside), with a troubled boy who called himself Jimmy after the recently deceased James Dean (he dropped me after a couple of dates, my first heartbreak, but Louise eventually married his best friend) and finally with John, who was my boyfriend for the next three years and with whom I discovered the pleasure and the boredom of requited love. But John is not really part of this picture (though he may be part of a bigger picture) and neither is Tooting Bec Lido, though I did go back there several times in the summer of 1990 to swim. It wasn't like swimming in the Mediterranean, but it provided its own distinctive, chilly pleasure, while the smell of chlorine brought back memories from 40 summers past.

Discovered that A.L. had been made Head of Features and Arts.

⌒

This is a reference to events in my old department at the BBC World Service. It was significant in the long run, because some years later A.L. gave me a job, and then I became Head of Features and Arts myself; at the time, his promotion was of only passing interest.

Tuesday 5th June

Read Peter's book – Sandstorms *– and slept early.*

⌒

Peter is my brother-in-law, the youngest of Paul's siblings. I had known him since he was ten; now he was a writer and Arabic scholar.

Wednesday 6th June

The gas man came.
    I worked in a desultory way. Paul rang to say he liked my Hardy programme.

⌒

Forget the gas man. Paul's phone call, encouraging and appreciative, revived my sense that he was the one person in the world who understood and cared about what I did. Talking to Paul was like talking to myself; we used words that no one else knew, laughed at unnamed memories, shared the network of associations that sprang to the other's mind at the mention of a person or place. Every phone call like this convinced me that one day we would be together again.

Friday 8th June

Went to Polegate on the train and visited my parents. We had a pub lunch at The British Queen. My father seems very old and frail but in good spirits. I got home around 6.30.

⌒

My parents knew that Paul and I had separated but I hadn't explained why. My family isn't good at that kind of conversation. Sometimes I wished I had a different family – a mother who would wrap me in her arms and cry with me, a father who would track Paul down and demand that he should return. It was an unreasonable expectation, considering their age – my father was in his mid-eighties. And I had told them so little about why Paul had left, precisely because I feared an emotionally charged encounter, even as I yearned for it. However, talking about dull everyday things over a ploughman's lunch – the Royal Family, why the milkman had left only one pint this morning when the indicator on the little milk crate had been set to two, whether the Stilton was better than the Cheddar and why they always gave you too much (my mother was seriously disturbed by abandoned food and believed that the main object of having a meal was to leave a nice, clean plate) – these conversational rituals provided an assurance that the world had not come to an end.

Saturday 9th June

I attended a one-day seminar to find out about training to be a counsellor. The rather po-faced proceedings were livened up by one of the participants, who believed in pleasure therapy i.e. sexual freedom and I suspect orgies and who challenged the counsellors on their assumption that monogamy was the natural order of things. One of them acknowledged that many people were involved in extra-marital relationships but said that those making up these triangles, quadrangles, whatever, didn't usually come for counselling together!

⌒

Two months before, while making the programmes about Thomas Hardy, over breakfast in a hotel in Dorchester, I had read an article in *The Guardian* about a training programme in couple counselling: a Foundation course and then a Diploma Course which would qualify its graduates for paid work as counsellors. I had written for further information and been invited to an Open Day.

About twenty women and three men were gathered in a well-proportioned room in a tall building in central London. Some of the faces would become familiar in time; one of them I knew already, though at first I couldn't remember why.

'Don't I know you?' we both said, as we filled our cups at the coffee urn and then I realised who she was.

'You're Michael's wife! Oh, I'm sorry. That's not how I should describe you.'

'That's all right. It's how you know me.'

Michael was a colleague at the BBC. We had been to dinner at their house and they had come to ours. I knew she worked for the Foreign Office. What was she doing here? It occurred to me that the most likely reason for wanting to become a couple counsellor was because your own marriage had gone wrong. That was why I was here.

We had lunch together in a nearby pub and both of us came up with other reasons for our presence. 'The article in *The Guardian* caught my interest; you never know when you might need another skill; you must keep your career options open.' I didn't tell her Paul and I had separated and she said nothing about her own marriage. Much later I discovered that her husband was having an affair with another woman.

I described the proceedings as po-faced, but I can't remember much of what we did because it has become confused with many similar occasions. Needless to say, we discussed the nature of marriage and relationships, giving the guru of sexual pleasure his chance to expatiate on the benefits of free love (the counselling professionals seemed more exasperated than shocked by this) and we watched a video of a counselling session. I think it was on this day, though it may have been later, that I first took on board a piece of information which should help make the picture clearer, if I can get it right. It goes something like this: the selection of a partner is governed by an unconscious choice mechanism which unerringly brings you together with a person whose strengths and weaknesses fit yours (like Barbara Cartland's notion of finding the other half of your soul). It's not simply that the partners complement each other; it can be a way of trying to get rid of a part of yourself, by handing it over to the other – so a secretly angry person, in order to remain calm and kind, chooses a very angry partner who will rant and shout for both of them. Unfortunately Mrs Calm may become exasperated with her ranting husband, especially as deep down, guiltily, she longs to shout and hurl abuse herself. So she punishes him, while his gentler feelings get buried deeper and deeper. Understanding this would be part of learning to be a counsellor.

Sunday 10th June

The Worgans came for lunch. David annoyed me by criticising the front door lock.

⌒

The Worgans again. The new door lock had been fitted because my key had been in the purse which was stolen as I left for Crete. My brother-in-law shook the door and said the workman had done a poor job. He expressed this vehemently, as was his way, and I was upset. A detailed account of the incident would be out of place here. Perhaps I'll come back to it.

Wednesday 13th June

Worked.
Marcel rang.

⌒

Marcel was still in America, coming to the end of the first year of his MA at Yale and planning to travel in the Soviet Union. Today was his birthday. He and his brother were, without question, the most important people in my life.

Twenty-two years earlier, after a long and frightening labour, I had looked at his small, mottled body and crumpled face, confident in the knowledge that he was the most beautiful and talented child there had ever been and that it was my privilege and duty to ensure that his genius flourished. Paul, who was present at the birth, felt the same.

Poor, first-born child! Saddled with such high expectations and invested with so much hope, Marcel was more than game for the impossible challenge, reading before he started school, always coming top of his class, getting As at O level and A level, a first at Cambridge and a scholarship to Yale. I fear he paid a high price in anxiety and suffered inordinately when he felt he wasn't the best in the universe. Our ambitions were never spelt out, or even consciously acknowledged. Later, when he rebuked me, as children do when they grow up, for making punishing demands on him, I felt I had to defend myself.

'But I always told you, I wouldn't mind if you were a dustman, as long as you were a happy dustman.'

'I knew you didn't mean it.'

I thought I did. I thought I was avoiding the mistakes of my own parents, who had made huge demands on me, the first surviving child in the family, a substitute son after an older brother died at birth. Their palpable pride when I excelled at school and won a place at Oxford became a scourge when I did less well. Again, this was never spelt out.

'Of course we're not disappointed. We just don't want *you* to be disappointed.'

'No, I'm not disappointed. I don't care. I didn't expect to get a first and it doesn't matter anyway.'

Someone wasn't telling the truth.

When Marcel read a book called *The Drama of Being a Child* by Alice Miller, he was convinced it was about him. He said that Paul and I had *narcissistically cathected* him. I read the book and thought my parents had done the same to me. It's like the famous Philip Larkin poem: *they narcissistically cathect you, your Mum and Dad, They do not mean to but they do ...* It means you treat your children as extensions of yourself and meet your own needs through them.

At 22, Marcel was still trying to be what he thought we wanted him to be and doing it brilliantly. It would take some time for him to enjoy being himself. Meanwhile, his estranged parents were not much help to him.

Interviewed Robin Hanbury-Tenison at Survival International.

⌒

Robin Hanbury-Tenison talked about the Yanomami tribe, who probably don't make these mistakes in bringing up their children. They have other, far worse things to worry about.

Dinner with D.F. at La Petite Auberge.

⌒

This was a friend from university days. We met towards the end of my second year (his third) and got on well. He marked the way for my career, going first to Nigeria with Voluntary Service Overseas and then coming back to work for the BBC, by which time I had been posted to Kenya by VSO. While I was in Nairobi, my friend, who came from the Midlands, lodged with my parents for a few months and commuted to the BBC until he was ready to set himself up in a flat. This had given him insights into my family which endeared him to me for ever. He teased my mother for insisting that saucepans stored upside down on the shelf need a space left 'so they can breathe'; he questioned the necessity of providing fish knives and forks from the canteen of best cutlery in order to eat sardines on toast (my mother protested that this was to prevent the normal knives and forks acquiring a fishy smell, but he demonstrated, by asking her to sniff the fish knives and forks, that this would not happen); he assured my parents that it was not imperative to unplug the television every night 'in case of fire'. Whether he was right about these things or not, he later became Head of Science at the BBC. Around the time that I got married, he got married too. Around the time that my marriage ran into difficulties, his did too and we met and exchanged confidences. He pioneered another path for me, when he went first for marriage counselling and then for personal therapy and analysis.

This relationship seemed to work best as a friendship – something to be picked up when it suited both and dropped when we were busy, with no betrayals and no hurt feelings, as far as I know.

There is an exercise used by family therapists (and sometimes couple counsellors) which involves arranging stones to represent people and their relationships, so in a conventional nuclear

Paul aged 25, at the time we met, in 1967. He was a lecturer in extramural studies at Makerere University, Kampala.

Soon after meeting we travelled through western Uganda, visiting some of Paul's long-distance students. In this picture I am in a dug-out canoe on Lake Bunyonyi.

Our wedding took place in Kampala registry office
on 4th December 1967.

Happy couple.

Paul, Gene and Alex Theroux, outside the White House in Washington, on my first visit to America, 1968.

On the Staten Island ferry, New York.

Paul and I on the steps of the Capitol.

Paul and Marcel,
soon after his birth
in Mulago Hospital,
Kampala, June 1968.

A new family of
three. (Taken by Priya
Ramrakha, friend and
photojournalist,who
died later that year while
covering the Biafran war.)

Paul in rural Uganda
with Marcel.

A strange group of extended family walking on Tooting Bec Common after lunch at my parents' house, on our stop in London before moving to Singapore: Alex's girlfriend Julie, my sister Ros, her husband Henry, Paul and Alex – and Marcel in his pram.

Marcel and I soon after our arrival in Singapore.

Marcel in the swimming pool in Singapore.

Marcel greets
his new brother,
Louis, born
20th May 1970.

Louis takes his first steps.

A family of four,
Singapore, 1970.

Singapore
friends.

Marcel, Susan, Ai Yah, Louis and Paul.

Anne Theroux 講師

My photo on the staff list of Nanyang University.

Paul and the boys, in Singapore.

After settling in London in 1972, I leave for work from our house in Catford. Catherine looks after the boys.

Paul at his desk with Louis (left) and Marcel (right). (Photo by Jerry Bauer.)

Relaxing with my sons.

A rare visit from V.S. Naipaul to our house in Wandsworth.

Paul and the boys at my parents' home in Dorset.

Marcel with his parents.

Self-portrait by Louis, given to me for Christmas 1986. He was sixteen.

The Theroux family, on Cape Cod. Paul is in the front with his sisters, Ann Marie and Mary. Brothers Gene, Joseph, Peter and Alex are in the back row, left to right. Mr and Mrs Theroux are between rows, to the right.

Paul rowing off Cape Cod.

Our family on the beach.

Louis and Marcel
on the Cape.

The Dike Bridge, Chappaquiddick.

Paul, Louis and
cousin Justin (in
the middle).

Louis and
Marcel with
their uncles.

Louis, Paul and Marcel on a trip to East Africa in 1984/5.

Family skiing.

Me with Bengt Danielsson, Kon-Tiki veteran and anti-nuclear lobbyist, at his house in Tahiti, 1988.

Paul and I making a series of radio programmes about crossing the Indian subcontinent by train 1985.

1987, Paul and I in Beijing in front of the Temple of Heaven.

On the road to Tibet.

In Lhasa, with the Potala Palace in the background.

1988, trekking in New Zealand.

In 1986 we travelled to Belize where *The Mosquito Coast* was being filmed.
This picture shows the Fox family, played by Helen Mirren and Harrison
Ford, Hilary and Rebecca Gordon, Jadrien Steele and River Phoenix.

Paul with director Peter Weir and the twins.

I watch the action, with Harrison Ford.

A reflective moment in
the Boboli gardens.

Paul and I started
1990 with a trip
to Florence. Paul
outside the Duomo.

In March I visited Eastern
Europe, first Budapest.

Then Prague, where this
red octopus in Wenceslas
Square symbolised the
collapse of communism.

Interviewing Gertrude Bugler, 'Tess of the d'Urbervilles', for a programme about Thomas Hardy, April 1990.

On a walking holiday in Crete, May 1990.

Visiting the palace of Knossos.

Poster advertising my interview with V.S. Naipaul at the National Theatre, September 1990.

family you would expect two stones together, husband and wife, with more stones at different distances representing children, other relatives and friends. It's a way of getting clients to talk about the bonds in their family. I was now a single stone. Around me was a large and straggly circle of friends, which sometimes overlapped with a tighter circle made up of my parents, my sister, her husband and children. Closest of all were my two sons. Next to me was an empty space.

Sunday 17th June

Drove to Oxford to collect Louis. We had a nice lunch, then I went to the Ashmolean and looked at the Minoan stuff and bought a book about Knossos.

Presumably Louis was packing while I went to the museum – or did he and Susanna come with me? I can't remember. He was twenty, in his second year at Magdalen, reading History and writing excoriating film reviews for an alternative undergraduate paper. ('Take your Walkman and a good book,' one of them concluded.) My diary shows that he often came back to London during term time, my memory tells me it wasn't often enough. This time he was coming back for the summer vacation.

Louis was born in 1970 after an easier labour than my first, which had taken me by surprise with its painful intensity. I was better prepared for the second and during it I performed breathing exercises, designed to achieve an ever-more shallow intake of air as labour progressed through its stages, thus reducing pain. It should have culminated in the soundless singing of 'Bye Bye Blackbird' (my choice of song; others can work just as well). The method was advocated in a book on natural childbirth, the bible of the antenatal class I signed up for in Singapore. The author was a midwife who was later discredited. For three quarters of the labour, trying to remember the exercises proved an effective way of taking my mind off the pain. But eventually the contractions became much more painful than the book or classes had led me to expect, and I found relief in voicing the words of my song defiantly. I like to think that Louis was born as I sang (or yelped) *where somebody waits for me, Sugar's sweet, so is he, Bye bye blackbird*. That would tie in with the *amah*'s explanation of why he was bitten by mosquitoes far more often than other children:

'Lulu very sweet', said Ai Yah, dabbing his legs with Tiger Balm ointment.

He was a large, placid and unassuming child.

'He'll make a good policeman,' said the doctor, looking at the scales.

In the noisily air-conditioned bedroom (the only room with an air conditioner in our house off Bukit Timah Road) Marcel recited nursery rhymes and confounded me with precocious questions.

'What that man's name?' (pointing at a photo in a newspaper).

'Tunku Abdul Rahman.' He was the Malaysian premier.

'Why that man's name is Tunkyabbyramy?'

I thought hard. 'Why is your name Marcel Theroux?'

He didn't pause for long. 'Because it isn't Tunkyabbyramy.'

Louis looked on and laughed. He took longer than his brother to learn to walk, talk and read, and my mother, who met him for the first time when he came back to England at eighteen months, said kindly, 'I expect he'll be good with his hands.'

Easy-going at home, he became boisterous and unruly at school, according to some teachers' accounts; I never really believed them. He surprised many people (though not me) when he got exam results that were as good as his brother's. He was very tall and had a tiny girlfriend whom he had known since schooldays and who was clever and funny like him.

Sunday 24th June

Went to Mavis MacLean's house for a St Hilda's reunion lunch.

⁓

I wasn't as happy as I should have been at university, (though I wouldn't have missed it, given the choice again) and I have mixed feelings about reunions. I hadn't much enjoyed a meeting in March when everyone seemed to be doing much better than me. But this was an informal lunch for women from my year (1962) with whom I had been friendly and I definitely wanted to be there. It was 25 years since I had seen some of the other guests; now in one brief conversation, balancing our plates of food, we swapped life stories. I had to impart the information that I had married Paul Theroux, lived with him in Africa, Singapore, Dorset and London, spent each summer on Cape Cod with him, raised two children who were both at university and had separated from my husband nearly six months ago. It wasn't as hard as I had feared; these women were sympathetic but not nosy; they too had experienced the revenges brought in by the whirligig of time: big ones like death and divorce; smaller disappointments like careers not commensurate with early talent, dull husbands, fading looks.

One or two male friends joined the party, including, late in the afternoon, a poet I had loved in my second year at Oxford, who was now living with a friend of a friend. Falling in love with writers seems to be part of the pattern of my life.

Monday 25th June

A blank! Did I do nothing on this day? Unlikely. So we must conclude the diary does not tell the whole truth. And perhaps I should point out that I have withheld some of the information entered on other days: interviews at Bush House, hours spent editing tapes, visits to Sainsbury's, meetings with friends, appointments at the doctor and the dentist. These entries have been discarded because they are boring, unimportant or don't fit the picture. Perhaps I should have discarded more. But not the Worgans.

Saturday 30th June

Worgans for dinner.

The diary shows that on 2nd June, 30th June and several times in between, I had meals with my sister and her family:

David, her second husband and Sam and Max, their sons, who reminded me powerfully of Marcel and Louis ten years earlier. Usually I went to their house, occasionally they came to mine.

When I wrote on Sunday 10th June, *The Worgans came for lunch. David annoyed me by criticising the lock on the door*, the diary entry was an understatement and an obfuscation. My brother-in-law had looked at the new lock, jiggled the door to prove that it didn't fit properly and clucked disapprovingly with the exasperated and yet triumphant air of a man who expects women to make a hash of such things.

'Fucking cowboys really took you for a ride.'

It was too much. I snatched the swear word and flung it back.

'Well, what the fuck am I supposed to do?' I shouted, in a way which alarmed the children (Sam, Max and Louis) and embarrassed my sister and me.

I suppose I was angry with Paul for leaving me unprotected and angry with myself for feeling that way. My question was not just about the door lock. What the fuck was I supposed to do?

Paul had been the centre of my life. He had appeared magically in Africa in his white suit when I was struggling to find my way, feeling that great things were expected of me but uncertain how to achieve them, whatever they might be. I sensed this man could achieve them for me and that all he wanted in return was a pretty girl who would applaud him and love him. He got more than he bargained for – a woman who insisted on a life of her own and shouted when she was thwarted and while that must have been disconcerting, I liked to think, and sometimes believed, that there were compensations. Over the years we had quarrelled, been unfaithful and hurt each other. We had also raised two children, laughed a lot, talked a lot and forgiven a lot. We had shopped together, cooked each other meals, comforted each other when life was hard, planted roses in the garden. For me, there was no other man. I had never envisaged a life without Paul; I couldn't envisage it now, even though the six months of our separation were almost over and neither of us had suggested how or when we might get back together.

I could make no picture without him. There were only fragments, meaningless stones.

Chapter 9

July

Sunday 1st July

Saw Lord of the Flies.

⌒

In this new film version, the shipwrecked schoolboys who become savages were played as American military cadets. It wasn't as good as the black-and-white film Peter Brook made in the sixties, but it conjured up that question about human beings – are we intrinsically evil? – which blasted through my head like a vacuum cleaner, disposing for a while of the cobwebs of self-pity. Don't worry, I have no intention of pursuing this one or even hinting at an answer, but by chance the month begins and ends with William Golding, who thought we were.

It was a hot summer. By July, the garden, pretty in May and early June, with the wisteria and clematis in flower, was parched and the white roses arching over the path had mildew. Normally at this time of the year I would be looking forward to Cape Cod, hunting for beach clothes in the summer sales, working long hours at my editing machine to earn the surge of liberation which comes when the jumbo jet breaks through the clouds and the drinks trolley clatters in the aisle. There was no flight booked to the States this year, though I hoped Paul might want me to visit him – or better still, might visit me. After all, the six months were up.

He was travelling again. Letters and postcards arrived regularly, from San Francisco, Australia, Tahiti, Fiji and Hawaii – but never from Los Angeles, where he had said the other woman lived. Perhaps she was no longer in the picture. He assured me that he loved me, missed me and wanted us to be together. I chose to believe him, deliberately not asking myself

'Why doesn't he do something about it?' The answer was too frightening to contemplate.

Why didn't *I* do something about it? I could have insisted on a meeting, said 'I want to see you, I must see you.' We would have met, hugged and laughed as we had done in April. Then he would have left again. And so the seesaw would continue – the elation of meeting and loving and then the thud of departure. Paul's *modus amandi*.

Freud believed that love and work are the driving forces of our lives. I have found work more constant. More controllable too. Presumably Freud wasn't thinking of a nine-to-five job in the office, but even that has its advantages. Getting a job had lifted my dejected spirits on two occasions in my life. The first was in Singapore when Marcel was small and I believed that I had blown my chances of success in the world for ever and become a downtrodden housewife like my mother. I was offered a job teaching English to Chinese students at Nanyang University. It was language teaching, not literature, but I was called a lecturer and immediately felt bigger and better. Three years later, back in England, after a few months of nappy-washing my self-esteem plummeted to drudge level. I applied for teaching jobs and was rejected. 'Who will look after your children?' asked the elderly, male principal of a College of Further Education. 'It is not our policy to recruit married women for overseas posting,' said the British Council, in a letter turning me down. Then I answered an advertisement for a job as a BBC World Service producer, to make radio programmes teaching English to foreigners. The more I found out about the work, the clearer it became that the post was made for me; given that life was turning out to be unfair, this didn't mean that I would get it. Marcel says he remembers me opening the letter of acceptance in the kitchen of our rented flat in Ealing and bursting into tears.

And so, for the next fifteen years, I was a staff producer at the BBC. It was rather like being back at school, with a variety of lessons on the timetable and praise for those who did well at them. Some of the lessons were tedious (but possibly good for you) and others interesting. The familiar structure felt safe. My career path didn't lead upwards, but outwards in ever-widening circles as I moved from language teaching, to books, to arts, to current affairs. Finally I felt strong enough to leave the BBC and become a freelance broadcaster. That had been three years ago and the decision had been made partly (only partly, mind) to allow me to spend more time with Paul. I would not have left the staff job had I foreseen our separation. The freelance life is a risky one. Being dropped as a presenter of the Radio 4 arts programme had hurt me. I was already thinking about more secure options, even while I was engrossed in work I truly enjoyed.

Friday 6th July

Put together Meridian Reports:

William Tell

Lord of the Flies

Dick Tracy

A rotten piece from Edinburgh on a play about dissident weavers who were hung, drawn and quartered.

A new Peter Barnes play.

Meridian Reports was the edition of the World Service arts programme which provided a round-up of news and reviews across the spectrum of the arts. *William Tell* was the Rossini opera. *Dick Tracy* was the movie with Warren Beatty. I can't remember what the Peter Barnes play was, let alone the one in Edinburgh. Other films I saw this month: *Windprints* (I interviewed the South African director); *Presumed Innocent* which was based on a novel by Scott Turow and *Trop Belle pour Toi* starring Gérard Depardieu. Other plays: *Earwig* at The Barbican left few impressions, though I discussed it on air in another edition of *Meridian* with the critic Michael Billington, who also recommended a new production of *King Lear* at Stratford.

For book programmes, I interviewed authors Edna O'Brien, Ruth Rendell, Mike Phillips, Tom Sharpe and Erica Jong. The last spoke about her new book, *Any Woman's Blues*. I liked her better than I thought I would and hoped she hadn't made the connection between me and Paul, who had savagely reviewed her first novel, *Fear of Flying*, when it was published in the early seventies.

Sunday 8th July

Worked on 'Native Americans'.

⌒

This was for *Endangered People*, the series at the moment closest to my heart. It was about tribal people whose once-strong identity was under threat. 'Tribal life is not just very fulfilling, it is very interesting,' said Robin Hanbury-Tenison, 'and the Yanomami were very, very fulfilled people for whom I had a huge admiration. They had no admiration for me and for other outsiders at all. For them the only possible thing to be is a Yanomami.' Yanomami life was shattered in the 1980s when 50,000 desperate *garimpeiros* (illegal miners) invaded the Brazilian rainforest looking for gold, bringing in return malnutrition, malaria and the destruction of one of the world's most perfect ecosystems. The Bushmen of the Kalahari were also in danger of extinction. Australian Aborigines, the Inuit and Native Americans were no longer in physical danger but had lost much of their traditional way of life. The Maori, I discovered, were fighting back, fiercely and successfully for education, jobs and land, while at the same time re-learning their half-forgotten chants and dances. They were having it both ways, as you must, to survive.

I had some fine expert speakers: as well as Robin Hanbury-Tenison on the Yanomami, the series included interviews with Robyn Davidson on Australian Aborigines, Hugh Brody on the Inuit and Laurens van der Post on the Bushmen of the Kalahari. But I needed the views and voices of endangered people themselves – without them the programmes would sound like westerners being romantic – and I had no budget for travel. Working for the impoverished BBC World Service required ingenuity at times like this.

A colleague visiting Australia recorded an aboriginal spokesman. An obliging Inuit went into a studio in northern Canada to be interviewed down the line about hunting whales and seals. A freelancer in South Africa tracked down a Bushman, who spoke in his own language in a very poor-quality recording, which I used sparingly. London's Maori society welcomed me to a meeting in New Zealand House where businessmen shed their suits to stamp out fierce dances and chant about their '*waka*' – the canoes which brought the original Maoris to Aotearoa, Land of the Long White Cloud, or as some wag put it (was it Paul or was he quoting someone else?) Land of the Wrong White Crowd. Now I needed a Native American and I happened to read, in *Time Out* I think, that a shaman called Winterhawk would be running a workshop in Tooting on links between Apache lore and Arthurian legend. I rang and arranged to interview him.

Winterhawk and I did not get along. He seemed put out. He insisted we sat on the living room floor and when I switched on my recorder and held out my microphone, saying 'Would you start by telling me your name?' he said, 'Don't you know my name?' as though I had insulted him. I switched off the machine.

'Yes, I do know. But I want you to say it on the tape. You see, I may not introduce you in the piece. I may just let you speak. So I want you to say, "My name is Winterhawk. I'm an Apache shaman." Then everyone knows.'

He shrugged and then said, 'What's the hurry? Why don't you tell me about yourself?'

'It doesn't matter about me. I'm just a journalist. I want to hear about you.'

It was hard work. He resented me and felt I was exploiting him. He told me angrily to 'relax', to 'communicate', to 'share'. Eventually, reluctantly, he told me that he belonged to a sub-tribe of the Apache whose culture had never been documented. There was just a sentence in the history books saying they had existed. 'My father is the last full-blooded member of his race of people. When he dies, that's it.'

Reading those words now, I am moved. At the time, I was rather disappointed. Winterhawk was not an eloquent spokesman. Fortunately, the programme would also include readings from a speech made by Chief Seattle in 1854:

Every part of this earth is sacred to my people. Every shining pine needle, every sandy shore, every mist in the dark woods, every clearing and humming insect is holy in the memory and experience of my people; the sap which courses through the trees carries the memories of the red man ... The air is precious to the red man for all things share the same breath; the beast, the tree, the man – they all share the same breath. The white man does not seem to notice the air he breathes; like a man dying for many days, he is numb to the stench; but if we sell you our land, you must remember that the air is precious to us, that the air shares its spirit with the life it supports.

Now that was more like it. That was what endangered people were supposed to say.

Several years later I was shocked to discover that these words were not spoken by Chief Seattle in 1854 but written by a Californian academic in the 1970s.* Plain truth; pretty invention. The brazen world of reality, the golden world of poesy. I preferred the noble and romanticised Chief Seattle to surly Winterhawk, who made me sit on a grubby carpet in Tooting and was suspicious of me.

---

* Chief Seattle was a real Native American leader who made a speech in 1854 during negotiations with the Washington territorial governor. His actual words have been lost and there are many different versions of what he might have said.

*'True words are not fine-sounding; fine-sounding words are not true.'**

Sunday 15th July

My parents and the Worgans came for lunch. Told my mother the truth about why Paul and I split up. Called his parents in the US and told his mother too.

~

What was the truth?

This version was blurted out as we walked across the common after lunch. I had drunk a few glasses of wine and responded to the gentle pressure from my mother to tell her whether I had heard from Paul.

'Yes. He writes to me often.'

'And when do you think you'll see him?'

'I don't know.'

'We were so sorry you decided to separate.'

My next words tumbled out.

'He had another woman.'

'Oh darling. Perhaps it wasn't serious.'

'I don't know. It wasn't the first time.'

She was sad and silent. My father had never been unfaithful, though she had once been jealous of his friendship with a woman who sang with him in the church choir.

I thought, but did not say, that I had been unfaithful too. Live by the sword, die by the sword. I couldn't complain. And

* *Tao Te Ching* by Lao Tzu.

I shouldn't be shopping Paul to my parents. But later, when my visitors had left and I'd had another glass of wine, I felt glad I had shopped him and decided to do it again, so I rang his mother in the States.

'Anne, how are you?' She sounded truly pleased to hear my voice.

'I'm fine.'

'Will we be seeing you on the Cape this summer?'

'I don't know. That's up to Paul.'

'I know he misses you.' Suddenly the American-accented warmth struck me as insincere. I became chilly. This time I spoke deliberately.

'Really? But he had another woman.'

'Oh, Anne.'

'And it wasn't the first time.'

'I don't know what to say.'

'The thing is, I can't live like this anymore. It didn't matter so much when we were younger. But I'm 47. He's got to decide if he wants to stay with me or not.' That was what wronged wives were supposed to say, wasn't it?

'I agree with you.' There was no insincerity now on her side of the Atlantic. She sounded elderly and hurt.

Wednesday 18th July

Went to Portsmouth for interview at Highbury College of Technology.

~

VSO still hadn't found a suitable posting for me, so I had started making other applications. I looked in *The Guardian* every

Saturday and Monday and answered advertisements. One of them was for a job teaching radio in the Media Studies department of Highbury College. I discovered that I could get on the train at Clapham Junction – ten minutes' walk from where I lived – and be in Portsmouth in just over an hour. So I wouldn't have to move immediately, I pondered, as the train clattered through Surrey and Hampshire. 'I could live there,' I thought several times, looking at a cluster of houses surrounded by trees and fields.

It was the kind of selection process that takes all day. In the morning, the candidates (one of whom I knew; he was a former head of the BBC African Service – what was he doing here?) were shown around the building, trooping through lecture rooms and studios, trying to say intelligent things in case the person guiding us was taking note. After an awkward lunch, we each spent half an hour in front of a panel of interviewers who sat on a raised platform behind a desk. The chairman of the board looked down at me kindly but seemed puzzled by my application.

'You have worked in Africa and Singapore and made all these programmes for the BBC. Why do you want to come here?'

I said I was interested in local radio and in teaching young people and thought: *Because my husband has left me after more than twenty years; because I've got to do something; because before when I was unhappy, getting a job was the solution; because the countryside looked lovely from the train window; because I want a life.*

At the end of the day we were told no one had been appointed. Unsure whether this was better than being beaten by one of the others or the worst insult of all, I went back to London wondering (as I still do from time to time) what would have happened if I had got that job. Would I have moved to a village outside Portsmouth, bought a cottage and a cat, cultivated a herb garden, gone for walks, made friends with other teachers at the college? It wouldn't have been bad. Just the thought that there were other lives to live gave me hope. That was what I wanted: a complete new life that I could inhabit as I had once inhabited the old life, with Paul, Marcel and Louis. That or the old life back again. But that old way of life was already a memory, becoming hazier and rosier as time went by, like the hunter-gatherer idyll of tribal people, a fantasy which could impoverish or enrich the present.

Monday 23rd July

Catching up – I'm four weeks behind with this diary.

Tuesday 24th July

What did I do today? My appointments book says I interviewed (or met) someone called Susan Haver at 11.15 at Bush House – doesn't ring any bells.

Wednesday 25th July

I remember now that Susan Haver was my contact in Personnel. I went for a board for a six-month job training East European broadcasters.

Saturday 28th July

I received a letter saying I had got the job with World Service Training.

⌒

I had answered another advertisement in *The Guardian*, for a job at Bush House, the BBC World Service HQ between Aldwych and the Strand, the place where I had already spent most of my working life, both on the staff and as a freelancer. This job was in the Training Department, running courses about the British media for East European broadcasters. The contract was for six months, starting in September. It wasn't a new life at a stroke, but it sounded interesting. Talking with Polish journalists, taking them to see different newspapers and broadcasting organisations, chairing discussions with politicians and other public figures – I could enjoy that. Going to the office every day would make me more purposeful. It was quite well paid. It would give me time to gather my strength.

So I was now committed to a full-time job in September. During July I also signed up for a part-time course in couple counselling, which would start in January 1991. I had a stake in the future. Two stakes. Yet I still believed that at any moment Paul would beg me to go back to the old life with him – or even a different life with him. We had often talked about living in America; I could do that – not on Cape Cod, but in New York, San Francisco, Honolulu ... The affectionate letters and cards from the Pacific raised my hopes; the lack of any plan for reconciliation made me doubt.

I said the month began and ended with William Golding. On 31st July I was preparing to interview Penelope Lively for the World Service series *Good Books*. She had chosen Golding's novel *The Inheritors*, which is the one I like best after *Lord of the Flies*. It suggests that we are descended from a savage, morally degenerate type of humanoid, who wiped out their better, more spiritual neighbours. Hence man's intrinsic cruelty.

But perhaps men are more often cowardly than cruel.

Chapter 10

August

Wednesday 1st August

Good Books *with Penelope Lively. She chose* The Inheritors *by William Golding.*

⌐

Good Books was a series I invented for the World Service when I was on the staff. It ran for more than fifteen years. Now that I was freelance I was sometimes asked to present it, which meant interviewing a guest about a favourite book, and steering the conversation towards pre-selected, pre-recorded extracts – an exercise which sometimes proved as tricky as corralling an unwilling horse. Over the years, hundreds of distinguished guests had chosen hundreds of books. Peter Porter picked Byron's *Don Juan*; Margaret Drabble, *Frankenstein* by Mary Shelley; Ian Hislop, *A Good Man in Africa* by William Boyd; Chris Bonington, *Savage Arena* by fellow mountaineer Joe Tasker, who died on Everest in 1982. It was a simple programme, yet occasionally there were difficulties. Robert Maxwell selected a novel of dubious merit just published by his own company (this was disqualified), and Geoffrey Robertson QC maintained that his favourite book was a novel by his wife, Kathy Lette (this was allowed, provided he declared his connection with the author). Arthur Scargill talked enthusiastically about *The Ragged-Trousered Philanthropists* by Robert Tressell, submitted an expenses claim which shot the programme way over budget and refused all further interviews with the BBC until he was paid (it was during the miners' strike so he was much in demand). Someone very famous chose *War and Peace* but turned out not to have read it.

Penelope Lively posed no such problems. She was co-operative about talking in a suitable way for World Service (taking into account the cosmopolitan audience and the deficiencies of short-wave broadcasting) and quick to realise when my question was a signal to head towards an extract. It was a pleasure to hear her views on *The Inheritors*, which I discovered was Golding's own favourite.

Saturday 4th August

The Metcalfs came.
  Cooked chicken.

~

I had been alone in the house – Marcel was travelling in the Soviet Union, Louis was on a working holiday in Czechoslovakia – so I was glad when Peter, Ros, Jessica and Leo Metcalf turned up, even when Ros reminded me they were allergic to feathers so could they have sheets and blankets, not duvets on the beds? They had made me welcome twice in Africa, once in Swaziland in 1984, where Peter was the Head of the United Nations Development Programme in Mbabane and I was researching the role of women in development and again, several years later, in Burkina Faso, where I arrived to cover the Ouagadougou Film Festival. The adults seemed much the same each time we met, despite the intervening years, but the children had changed dramatically, from cuddly tots, to small, shy people who stiffened when I tried to hug them. On Sunday we all went together to The London Dungeon and looked at gruesome torture implements. After lunch they left by train for Scotland, to stay with another friend. Three of them had red, swollen faces because although I had provided blankets, not duvets, I had forgotten that some of my pillows were filled with feathers. We said goodbye at the station. Their next posting would be Madagascar. They hoped I would visit them. We hadn't talked about Paul. Ros had made one tactful inquiry and I had deflected her. Now I was sorry.

Driving home through the bad-tempered traffic and heavy heat, I envied Ros her young family, even if they did suffer from inconvenient allergies, and I envied Peter's job which took them to interesting places, where Ros would teach at the local university. My hopes of finding work abroad were fading, though not extinguished. There was still a glimmer of hope in the distance. But for the next six months, I would be working in London, in World Service Training. My contract ran from 10th September. I decided to take a short holiday in the Lake District in the first week in September and made a booking at a hotel on Derwentwater.

On 6th August Marcel arrived home from his travels in the countries still referred to then, but not for much longer, as the Soviet Union. On 9th August Louis returned from Czechoslovakia. My own family was almost complete. The heat seemed less oppressive as we sat in the garden discussing the world.

On 10th August I drove through Kent, looking at oast houses and stately homes with my friend Margaret Walters and a visitor from America; it was on that trip, using a phone in a roadside café, that I returned a call from a publisher who asked if I would like to chair a platform discussion with V.S. Naipaul at the National Theatre in September. I accepted.

'Which auditorium?' demanded Louis, when I got back and told them about the oast houses, the stately homes and the phone call. 'The Cottesloe?'

'The Olivier, actually.'

'Mum's riding high!' They both wanted me to feel better. When they were around, I usually did.

For a few weeks the house was full of laughter and arguments again. My sons' friends dropped in and joined us for impromptu meals. The phone rang. Louis' girlfriend, Susanna, often stayed. Like him, she was about to begin her third year at Oxford, reading History. I joined them at the table one morning as they ate tomatoes on toast – their breakfast, though for me it was nearly lunch time – and they told me they planned to visit America at the beginning of September; they were thinking of staying on the Cape with Paul for a while. They looked at me anxiously, gauging my reaction.

'Good idea. Give him my love.'

This ended a fantasy of mine that Paul might join me on my trip to the Lake District where we would climb Helvellyn together and talk about the future as we struggled upwards. I had no other plan that involved him and I had failed to find out what he was planning. The six months were up. What did he think? How did he feel? When we spoke on the phone he prevaricated. He promised that a letter with a proposal would arrive soon. It did, at the end of the month.

Wednesday 29th August

Got a letter from Paul which upset me – it suggested we planned outings or a trip rather than live together.

Evidently it had been a difficult letter to write; he said he had started several times, then torn the paper from the typewriter and started again. So I was ready for some hard truths.

He began with praise – thanks for my support and love and contribution to his success. This was at some length and written in the fluent words which were his gift and still had the power to please me, though I knew a *but* was coming.

He wondered if those great days were over and could not be recaptured; I had said some very hard things to him, in conversation and messages on the phone. (This was true. On several occasions I had rung and called him a bastard. Maybe worse things. But I had written passionate loving letters too. As he had.)

He ended with the proposal he had promised. Rather than plunging back into a shared life in London or on Cape Cod we should have a period of getting to know each other again, a return to our brief courtship in Uganda, in March, April and May 1967. He had nearly enough frequent flyer miles for two first-class tickets round the world. He would like me to go with him. Perhaps we could talk about it? He was sorry he couldn't come to the Lake District.

I didn't understand it. I re-read it several times. Sometimes it struck me as obvious that he was saying 'This is the end' in the kindest, cowardliest way possible. But I was unwilling to receive this information, and easily seduced by declarations of love, past and present, which seemed so real.

'He can't face my jealousy and anger,' I thought, regretting all the ugly outbursts. But how could I not be angry and hurt? It's the right of those who are betrayed. He had raged when I betrayed him and I had stood and borne the buffeting. Why could we not go through the process of anger, contrition and forgiveness? I could forgive, in time, if he were truly sorry. I could try to understand how I had failed him and do better. There was something missing from the picture.

I telephoned him and said I didn't think a round-the-world trip – even a first class one – was the answer. There was a pause. He retracted a little and said I had misunderstood him. I waited, hoping and yet dreading that we might start out on the painful, truthful dialogue that was the only way forward.

'Anyway, you're off to the Lake District. I don't suppose you'll see a host of golden daffodils …'

'Not likely in September.'

We resumed our affectionate banter. Later, alone, I felt despair.

On 30th August, Marcel left for the States and on 31st Louis and Susanna followed. The house was empty again.

Chapter 11

September

Saturday 1st September

Set out about twelve and drove to the Lakes.

My walking boots and the complete works of V.S. Naipaul were in the car, the poetry of William Wordsworth was in my head as I sped northwards.

> *What dwelling shall receive me? In what vale*
> *Shall be my harbour? Underneath what grove*
> *Shall I take up my home? And what clear stream*
> *Shall with its murmur lull me into rest?* *

In 1960 when I studied Wordsworth for A level, the English class was divided about him. Some girls said his poetry made a welcome change from T.S. Eliot's back alleys. Others of us strongly disagreed. Eliot was sad and cynical and suited our mood, even if he did join the Church of England. Some of the Romantics were OK but not Wordsworth. I was a Byron admirer myself and I liked the picture of him wearing an open-necked shirt and loose jerkin; one of my friends was passionately devoted to Shelley; Coleridge and Keats had their supporters too. We argued about our heroes rather as three years earlier we had discussed the strong points of Elvis, Cliff, Adam and Marty. It was hard to feel that way about William Wordsworth. His nose was too long and so were his life and work. But somehow, in the course of reading Books One and Two of 'The Prelude', we had a change of heart which we couldn't properly explain.

* 'The Prelude' Book 1.

'I thought you hated Wordsworth,' said one classmate suspiciously.

'Not anymore.'

'May we know why?'

'Had a revelation.'

'What do you mean, a revelation?'

'Well, a sort of vision.' I looked at my friend Olive and we both smiled in what must have been an irritating way.

'Where?'

'Streatham Common. On the way home after hockey practice.'

There was a grain of truth there. Olive and I and two or three others had been walking down the hill with our satchels hanging from our shoulders, feeling elated because rain had put a stop to the compulsory fooling in the mud with 22 sticks and one ball, when a serendipitous effect of light, colour and shade produced by the sun shining through wet leaves, had stirred us to quote aloud from the poet we despised. Our next essays were marked 'A', which seemed to validate the experience.

It was Wordsworth's mysticism that suddenly appealed to me, the Wisdom and Spirit of the Universe, not an old man with a beard, scowling down at us, but a *presence* in a world where the meanest flower might bring thoughts too deep for tears and a boy ran through fields trailing a kite. I decided that one day I would live in a cottage in the Lake District and give my children a Wordsworthian upbringing. This has not come about, though I did spend one short holiday there in 1964, with my sister, giving her a hard time as we climbed Great Gable in our plimsolls. Then came Africa, Singapore, marriage and children, who grew up mostly in south London, like me. Paul once went fishing in the Lakes with Jonathan Raban and Robert Lowell but I wasn't invited to accompany them.

Now here I was, staying at a hotel on the edge of Derwentwater, in a little village called Portinscale.

Sunday 2nd September

Explored Keswick, took the launch round the lake then walked along the shore.

Monday 3rd September

Climbed Latrigg – a small peak near Skiddaw and got wonderful views of all the main peaks.

⌐

For the first few days I walked alone, returning to the hotel to eat my dinner alone and read the work of V.S. Naipaul in my room. It was good. If you walk far enough you can leave your demons behind; demons don't like long walks, especially uphill. They lag behind, whingeing and eventually give up and slink away. Each day, after toiling upwards and arriving at a vantage point where the countryside was spread before me, I felt light and free.

But walking by yourself has disadvantages. You can get lost. You can get scared. You can feel lonely. You can spend more time poring over the map in a worried way than actually putting one foot in front of the other. It's better with a like-minded companion. Wordsworth had Dorothy and Coleridge.

I had nobody. So I joined a group of walkers who met each day at the Moot Hall in Keswick, first on a sunny, lakeside stroll, then on a trek through mist and rain to Dale Head Tarn and down again, soaking wet. Another day a National Park ranger came with us and explained the history of the Lakes, from their formation in the Ice Age to the present. There were traces of the past all around us, he said – axes and arrow heads and even a few strange words: the *Yan Tan Tethera* used for counting sheep. For once I had a pleasant sense of belonging to Britain with its ancient past. Normally I considered myself an outsider (though this was a state of mind; as far as I know my ancestors were Anglo Saxon) and most of the people I admired were outsiders too. Like V.S. Naipaul.

I travelled with him in the evenings, beginning with his latest work about India, *A Million Mutinies Now*, which was the peg for the discussion I was chairing in a week or so at the National Theatre. I liked the book, not least the picture of the author on the back cover with a notebook in his hand and a handkerchief on his head as protection from the sun. It was generous and capacious, a quest for understanding, a journey of the mind. It was not a travel book.

I had my doubts about travel books, for all kinds of reasons. Travel writing had brought Paul's first commercial success, but it had also brought separation and misunderstanding. Each journey had been hard for all of us. You know about the first one, *The Great Railway Bazaar* trip, during which I was unfaithful. The next big journey, to South America for *The Old Patagonian Express*, was probably the best absence. Paul grew a large moustache while he was away; the boys and I were snowed up for a week at my parents' house in Dorset; later he said in a radio interview 'I wished every day I was at home. I have a house in London and a very happy family – I didn't want to be away.' Yes, that was how it should be. I didn't mind him going away if he said things like that. It should have been all right the next time, when he travelled round England in 1982 for *The Kingdom by The Sea*, because he was able to come home at weekends, but it wasn't. By then he was dissatisfied with the marriage and with England and involved with the teacher in Pennsylvania. The bile in his portrayal of the British which many readers relished, spilled over into our home life. Or could it be the other way round? Did he dislike Britain because he was bored with his British life and his British wife? When he went to China in 1986 for *Riding the Iron Rooster*, he met up with the same woman, who was now teaching English in Shanghai, and they resumed their affair. Now he was in the Pacific for the book that would be published in 1992: *The Happy Isles of Oceania*. I haven't read it, though I know I'm mentioned in it. Nor have I read any of his later travel books. Perhaps I will one day. Unlike the general public, I prefer his novels. But I haven't read those since we parted either. I'm still afraid of words that will wound me.

A thought on travel. When Petrarch climbed Mont Ventoux in the south of France in 1336 he read a passage from the Confessions of St Augustine at the top: *'men go forth and admire lofty mountains and broad seas and roaring torrents and the course of the stars and forget their own selves in doing so.'* Petrarch went home, never described the view from the mountain and never travelled again, but whether that was because he was disillusioned or because he had received enough inspiration to last a lifetime, I don't know.

Thursday 6th September

Weather even worse so drove to Buttermere, then to Cockermouth but Wordsworth's house was shut. Bought some waterproof trousers. Started reading India: A Wounded Civilization.

⌒

This is Naipaul's second book about India and one I hadn't read before. The first was *India: An Area of Darkness*, published in the sixties, which I read on Paul's recommendation soon after we met. And now in 1990, he was about to publish a third, which was different; its mood, defiant not despairing, reflected in the title: *India, A Million Mutinies Now*.

Naipaul had hated India, his ancestral home, when he first visited it. He sometimes seemed to hate the West Indies where he had been born. He had certainly hated East Africa, which he visited in the 1960s. Now he lived in Wiltshire and seemed to like it. What was it about the English countryside that soothed the most troubled spirit?

Before I left the Lake District I collected some sheets from an estate agent giving details of houses for sale.

Saturday 8th September

Picked up Ann from her guest house and drove back to London.

⌒

We had met on a walk earlier in the week. She had been one of those who turned up at the Moot House each day. She was from Dublin, staying with a group of friends at a Catholic hostel. Instead of returning to Ireland with the others, she had decided to visit her daughter in Islington. On the journey she told me about her life. She was a widow. She had nine children and her husband had died when the youngest was four and the eldest seventeen.

'It must have been very hard to bring up nine children.'

She considered this. 'I think it gets easier. I thought the first one was hard work, and we were living in Africa and had servants at the time.'

'Whereabouts?'

'Uganda.'

'My first son was born in Uganda too.'

'Mulago hospital?'

'Yes.'

In that hospital, thousands of miles away on the equator, both of us had lain in labour. It had been a good hospital then, though later, in the bad years of Amin's rule, an elderly hostage was killed there, during the Entebbe Airport siege. Her name was Mrs Bloch. She was dragged down a flight of stone steps.

At some point on the M6 I told my companion I had separated from my husband after 22 years.

'When did you separate?'

'Last January.'

She was silent for a while.

'It's still very soon.'

Did this mean it would take me a lot longer to get over it? We were both quiet for many miles.

'It must have been very hard for you when your husband died.'

'It was,' she said. 'But I was so busy with the children that I didn't have time to get depressed.' After a few more miles she added, 'Some people say that death is easier to deal with than divorce.'

'I shouldn't think so,' I replied doubtfully. I was unwilling to claim that my loss could in any way be greater than hers.

I know now what I didn't know then, that the pain following a death is sharper because the knowledge you will never meet again is certain. But that mourning procession, however slow, moves steadily in one direction, whereas my journey of loss was full of stops and starts. Sometimes I strode forward alone, eager to reach a point where I could safely pause and look around at the view. Sometimes I got worried, turned and went back the way I had come.

Monday 10th September

Started work in Training at Bush House.

⌒

I was the co-ordinator of a course for six Polish broadcasters who were due to arrive the following Sunday, one of a series funded by the Foreign Office for East Europeans. There were two other people in the office. Klara, a beautiful Hungarian, was running a course for her compatriots which was scheduled to start in a few weeks. George, who was 22 and had been at school with my son, Marcel, spent much of the time perched on a high stool in front of a computer, in the posture of a

Dickensian clerk, with hunched shoulders and raised elbows and knees, surrounded by a mess of papers and leaflets. I'm not sure what his job title was. When the Head of Training put her head around the door and shouted 'George!' he would sit up straight and blink anxiously.

'Could you move the overhead projector into G45?'

'Yes, of course, certainly.' George had mastered the trick of sounding genuinely happy to obey. 'Would you like me to do it before I take the information packs to the British Council?'

'Haven't you taken them yet? Could you move the projector *now*, darling? It's a tiny bit crucial. Then get the packs to the Council.'

'Now it is, then,' and George would spring into action, tipping yet more papers onto the pile on the floor.

There was a whiff of panic in the room.

Sunday 16th September

In the evening George and I met the Polish broadcasters at the St Giles Hotel for a drink.

~

The St Giles Hotel is another name for the YMCA near Tottenham Court Road. Andrzej, Grażyna, Idalia, Lesław, Marek and Paweł (whose names and faces we had memorised from the photos attached to their applications) had been selected to spend six weeks in Britain, learning how the media operate in a democracy. They would visit newspapers and broadcasters in different parts of the country, but first they would be briefed in London.

The Head of Training had devised an excellent programme. There was a visit to Parliament, dinner with MPs, a talk by a high-ranking police officer and the chance to go out in a panda car. She said the course must not be a propaganda exercise, and there was a detailed discussion of the Thames Television documentary, 'Death on the Rock', about how British security forces shot down three unarmed IRA members in Gibraltar: the government had attempted unsuccessfully to ban the programme and Rupert Murdoch tried to discredit it in his newspapers. In another session we showed gruesome television footage of maimed bodies, casualties of a bomb explosion, and discussed whether it was right to broadcast such pictures. What are the limits of freedom and truth? The Poles, it turned out, didn't have high expectations of either. They were used to picking their way among distortions and propaganda, like shoppers in a store of shoddy goods, finding just enough to get by on.

It was an interesting course but inevitably some things went wrong. The video broke down. The sandwiches didn't arrive. One of the Poles swigged back a bottle of wine at lunch time and snored during the talk on Audience Research. Then a man from the Foreign Office turned up, uninvited, at a question-and-answer session with the BBC's media correspondent. The Head of Training, considering this an infringement of the corporation's independence, glared at him and did not offer a chair. On this difficult day, I had to leave the room punctually at 5.30pm to interview the novelist Nadine Gordimer about her latest book, *My Son's Story*. As I slipped out, I felt a fierce torch-beam of annoyance shift from the Foreign Office man to me.

Nadine Gordimer can also be fierce; she gave a sharp response to one of my questions which generalised about South

Africa from the people in the novel (most writers regard their fictional characters as unique one-off creations, not archetypes or representatives) but her spikiness was nothing compared with the displeasure I encountered at work next day from the Head of Training.

'I wish you hadn't done that.'

'What?'

'Leaving before the end. It looked so bad.'

'But I told you I had to interview Nad—'

'I wish you hadn't.'

I said nothing more. Her attitude was ominous. I had told her when I took the job that there were one or two existing commitments I couldn't abandon, and she had seemed to understand; now it appeared she hadn't. However, volatility rather than malice was her flaw and a few days later, when I asked if I could leave work half an hour early because I was chairing a discussion with V.S. Naipaul at the National Theatre, she simply nodded in a distracted way, as if she had never heard of him.

I hadn't heard of him myself before I met Paul at the Kampala Jazz club in 1967, but his name came up in our first, hurried conversation, which was conducted while my escort was in the toilet. By the time he came out, we had arranged to meet the following evening, outside the university library.

Paul arrived late and running. I was sitting on the steps in the sunshine, wearing a loose dress made of material with an African pattern which was actually manufactured in Indonesia. We went to the Speke Hotel, where we drank lager in the garden and resumed the conversation begun the previous night, about the writers we admired: Lawrence Durrell, Graham Greene, Chinua Achebe (me); Henry de Montherlant, S.J. Perelman, V.S. Naipaul (Paul). We both liked Milton, John Donne, Coleridge and T.S. Eliot. Paul was not as keen on Wordsworth as I was. Other literary names were bandied on that first date which culminated in a kiss in the car, and during our brief courtship; Naipaul was a constant companion.

He had visited Kampala the previous year. Paul had shown him some of his own writing and the older man (Naipaul was in his thirties) had been encouraging. Naipaul enjoyed phrases and *bons mots*, and on long car trips to remote areas Paul, who drove, (Naipaul couldn't or wouldn't) took many of them to heart. 'Naipaul says "Give no one a second chance. The man who lets you down once will let you down again."' Later I read this perception in *The Mimic Men*, the novel published in 1967 about the painful transition of a West Indian colony to independence. 'Naipaul says "Hate the oppressor, fear the oppressed."' That comes from the same book. 'Naipaul says "Art is long and life is short."'

'Didn't someone else say that first?'

'Yes, but that was in Latin.'

When Paul told me what Naipaul had said about Africa, I was puzzled. Had he really said, 'It's the ones with books that scare me'? or 'Promise me you will never write again' (to a student who showed him a manuscript)? Why did Paul find these comments amusing? He said Naipaul despised white liberals and had specially hated a gay man we both knew, an expert on African writing. (This particular character later appeared in Naipaul's novella about East Africa which won the Booker Prize in 1971, *In A Free State*.) I wasn't sure I liked the sound of V.S. Naipaul, but Paul admired him and I was in love with Paul so I tried to suppress my doubts.

Just a few months before he met me, Paul had stayed with the Naipauls in London. They had introduced him to people like Cyril Connolly, Francis Wyndham and Edna O'Brien. Did I know them? I said I didn't, though I knew their work. I told him I had once been interviewed by Iris Murdoch when I applied to read PPE at St Anne's where she was a Philosophy don, but that I ended up reading English at St Hilda's. Paul said approvingly:

'Pat Naipaul was at Oxford. That's where she and Vidia met. She did history.'

'What does she do now?'

'She looks after Vidia. She used to be a teacher at a girls' school; I think she was head of the history department. But she gave it up. He needed her at home.'

No, I wasn't sure I liked the sound of V.S. Naipaul, or his domestic arrangements, but then Paul gave me a copy of *Mr Stone and the Knights Companion*, the novel about an elderly Englishman who blossoms late in life and masterminds a scheme to turn pensioners into champions. I felt reassured. It was a funny and humane book. He must be all right.

'What did you think it was about?' Vidia Naipaul asked me, six months later when, newly married, we visited him and Pat at their flat in Stockwell. He had become suddenly serious, looking at me intently through hooded eyes. A moment before he had been laughing uproariously at one of his own *bons mots*, which Paul had recalled.

'I think it's about growing old ...' His expression, a puzzled wince, indicated that this was not the response he had hoped for and I tailed off.

I wanted to say more – I had much more to say – but it was too late; the subject had been whisked away and another was in its place. I felt shy. It wasn't that I was stupid, I told myself, I just wasn't used to his way of talking. He seemed impatient and mocking. His wit and range of references excited me, but he laughed at serious things and was enraged by trivialities.

Pat Naipaul tried to put me at my ease, then and on other occasions. She was a kind woman with prematurely grey hair and a sweet face; she had come to my parents' house for the wedding party a few days earlier (Vidia had a previous engagement) and hadn't flinched at the noisy relatives who barracked my father and Paul during their speeches and drunkenly sang 'Why was he born so beautiful?' She gave us a green, linen tablecloth as a present.

'You mustn't be afraid to speak your mind,' she whispered to me once, after I had been silent throughout a dinner party. She was very intelligent, a solicitous hostess, had read what her husband read and knew about everything which preoccupied him. She always entered the conversation courageously, though once I saw her cry when Vidia dismissed what she said.

On this first evening with the Naipauls I was worried as well as overwhelmed. My father had bought tickets for the whole family to see Harry Secombe as Mr Pickwick in a musical and we had arranged to meet in the foyer. Paul seemed to have forgotten the time – he was enjoying the conversation too much. The hands of my watch were creeping towards the time we had agreed to meet. 'We ought to leave,' I muttered. The conversation continued and I felt angry, thinking of my father standing with the tickets in his hand, anxiously scanning the crowd. 'We must go,' I said, at last, trying to sound relaxed and good-humoured.

'What are you going to see?' Pat asked and Paul told her, apologetically. 'Anne's father chose it.'

'I've heard it's good,' said Pat. Vidia said nothing. I imagined that he sneered.

In the taxi Paul pressed me for my views on the Naipauls. 'They're very nice,' I said and he appeared satisfied. Meeting them was a challenge which by my own standards I had failed; but it seemed possible to pass the test by looking pleasant and smiling. That I can do, I thought. But is it really enough?

When we arrived at the theatre, fifteen minutes late, my father was waiting, cross and anxious as I knew he would be, and we slipped into our seats just as the curtain went up on Harry Secombe as Mr Pickwick, standing centre stage and singing about how joyful life would be, if he ruled the world.

Over the years I had read all Naipaul's books, carefully and suspiciously. I always admired them. We visited him and Pat from time to time, in Wiltshire where they bought a cottage in the early seventies and at their pied-à-terre in Kensington. As time went by, Pat grew tense and nervous and eventually became very ill. She came to dinner once or twice, but Vidia never joined us for a meal at our house. Paul said he was particular about his food because he was a Brahmin. I became less intimidated by his quirky, passionate manner, although I continued to be in awe of him. At first I believed that my wariness was because of his intellect and knowledge and the refinement of his taste (I remember looking with him through a magnifying glass at the details of a Mughal miniature he had bought); but there was something else in him which made me quail: a fierceness and contempt, a determination to strike first – I can't define it. And it could be that I'm not describing something in him, but something in me, a fearfulness that he evoked. Sometimes I felt it was the belief that Art is long and Life is short that worried me; it was a profound conviction that permeated everything he did and said. It was a dangerous belief. It could be used as an excuse to treat people badly. It was a belief I feared Paul shared. When Paul was obsessed by the English teacher in Pennsylvania and I was jealous and hurt, he asked Vidia what he should do. 'Go and live with this other woman,' was the advice he got. 'You must. Immediately.'

Meanwhile, since that first meeting, when I was just married, pregnant, self-conscious and far too sensitive about feeling unimportant (the insecurity of the young is part of their vanity), since then, more than twenty years had passed and I had grown up. I was no longer scared, even as I sat with Sir Vidia on the platform of the Olivier Theatre. Why should I be scared? These people had come to hear him, not me.

I explained to the audience that we had first met many years ago when I was already an admirer of his work but hadn't dared question him about it. Now was my opportunity, and theirs, to put whatever questions we wanted. Several hands went up. The first question was about India. He gave an interesting answer. We were off. The audience asked good questions; he treated them openly and fairly, still suffused by the optimistic mood of the book; the time flew by. Then a black man asked him about Africa; the optimism vanished and he said something dismissive;

the man challenged him; Sir Vidia started to get angry. I saw the lady from the National Theatre signalling that it was time to stop and I attempted some sort of summing up, thanking the guest and leading the applause.

'You were terrific,' I said as we came off stage.

'Was I all right?' He looked pained, then smiled as we all assured him he had been brilliant.

We were taken out to dinner. Around the table were publishers and theatre people, Gillon Aitken (Vidia's agent and Paul's), and a woman who arrived late and took the seat next to Vidia.

'This is Margaret,' he said. 'Margaret, this is Anne. Paul's wife.'

We shook hands.

'You weren't in the audience?'

'No I wasn't,' she glared, giving the impression that listening to Vidia talk about his writing was the last thing she would want to do. She seemed annoyed with him, pooh-poohing his opinions and ignoring his *bons mots*.

'I had hoped to see *Private Lives*. Joan Collins is in it.'

'I've heard it's good,' I said, and we had a conversation about Joan Collins, *Private Lives* and *Dynasty*.

Vidia put his hand on Margaret's arm in a placatory way and intimated he would take her to the play another night.

Afterwards I walked to Waterloo, passing the shacks of the men and women who lived in the Bullring. I had interviewed several of them for a programme about homelessness, heard their stories of hardship and misfortune, admired their resilience. Tonight I belonged to the world that existed above their hovels, the comfortable world of affluence, art and celebrity.

I decided to take a taxi. At home I summed up the evening in my diary:

Monday 24th September

Interviewed V.S. Naipaul at the National Theatre. I think it was OK.

~

September had been a good month. During its final days I accompanied the Poles on a short trip to Scotland, looked at tiles with a view to renovating the bathroom, had dinner with the Worgans and edited the interview with Barbara Cartland which I had recorded way back in May. All these activities were satisfying.

Chapter 12

October

Wednesday 3rd October

Took Poles to Radio 1, then by train to Birmingham.
Dinner with Roy Saatchi.

～

The Poles had been divided into two groups of three for accompanied visits to broadcasting stations in different parts of Britain. Birmingham and Glasgow were my destinations. In both places I was expected to offer modest hospitality to local bigwigs in return for information and access to their premises. Hence the dinner – curry I think – so that Roy would talk to the Poles about BBC Birmingham and allow them to spend the whole of the next day watching what went on there.

Thursday 4th October

Left Poles at BBC. Went shopping.

～

There was no point hanging around with them, like a mother who is reluctant to leave her children at school. But without Paweł, Marek and Grażyna to look after, in a strange city where I had no office, it was hard to decide how to spend my time purposefully. Modest, recreational shopping was one answer. I bought a nightdress and some shoes. Tomorrow shorter visits had been scheduled, to smaller stations, and I would accompany them.

Friday 5th October

Visited WM, the BBC local station, then BRMB, an independent station.

Train back to London.

~

Glasgow the previous week had been more fun. We had spent the first evening in the bar of the Grosvenor Hotel with Jack Regan, a man with a mission to enlighten Eastern Europeans about Scotch whisky and Scottish nationalism, and members of his newsroom staff who fancied a free drink. One young man made a bit of an ass of himself quite early in the evening by praising Marxism: he said the only reason it hadn't worked in Poland was because they had adopted a Leninist model. I already knew after a week with the Poles that they didn't like Marx. They didn't like communism. They didn't like socialism. They liked capitalism and Mrs Thatcher, the latter fervently. They told everyone they met how wonderful she was and looked surprised and slightly hurt when we were not suitably gratified. Now the tables were turned and the Poles put the young Trotskyist firmly in his place: he had never lived under Marxism; he didn't know what he was talking about; it did not work.

About Scottish nationalism they were open minded, though rather surprised by Jack's vehemence, which increased as the evening went on.

'You said England!' he roared, overhearing part of a conversation in which, to the best of my recollection, I had used the word quite appropriately.

'Sorry. Should I have said Britain?'

'That's typical! But we're used to it.' He addressed the Poles. 'They probably haven't mentioned this on the course you're doing in *London*,' (with a sneer as if he were speaking of Gomorrah), 'but if you listened only to Radio 4 and the BBC's other so-called national networks, you wouldn't know there was anything north of St Albans, let alone a country called Scotland with its own laws and its own educational system.'

This went on for some time, and he contrived to interweave the lecture with a demonstration of the subtle distinctions between different malt whiskies. The Poles enjoyed the lesson, which involved frequent calls to the barman, and at the end of the evening I picked up a large tab, payment in advance for the next day, when Jack would find them a place in his busy news room, leaving me free to admire the architecture of Charles Rennie Mackintosh and the shops in Sauchiehall Street. The day after that we visited Scottish TV and Radio Clyde before flying back to London.

Two weeks later I made exactly the same visit with the second group of Poles, Lesław, Andrzej and Idalia. The young Trot didn't show up in the bar of The Grosvenor, but everything else was as before.

It was a month of getting on trains and planes, unpacking in hotel rooms, meeting people and being polite, keeping the conversation going when an awkward silence fell, glossing over the Poles' occasional lapses in tact ('But why is your equipment so old fashioned?') and feeding them the prompt lines which I hoped would make them say interesting things.

'Lesław has a story about Lech Wałęsa.'

'Andrzej made a film about Kim Il Sung.'

'Grażyna comes from Łódź.'

'None of them thinks much of Gorbachev.'

Then I would arrive back in London, opening the door of my house with caution, because the hall was full of debris and there was a strange man working there.

Saturday 6th October

Bought floor tiles.

~

I was having the bathroom refurbished.

After Paul left I had become conscious of signs of neglect in the house. When we had first moved in, with little money but lots of energy, we had scrubbed and painted and made improvements, chipped the plaster off the chimney breast and lined the living room with tongue-and-groove wood panelling. It's what young married people do – what Larkin calls '*A joyous shot at how things ought to be.*'*

I sat at an old sewing machine making curtains; Louis held the material straight and I turned the handle, hoping the ancient contraption would complete the line of stitching without going mad and producing a frenzy of tightly tangled thread – as it did from time to time. Afterwards we both developed rashes on our hands from the cheap, synthetic material.

As time went by, although in theory there was more money to spend, we lost the will to make improvements. We tolerated

* 'Home is so Sad' by Philip Larkin. Reprinted with permission of Faber and Faber Ltd.

defects that had once bothered us. We failed to notice that things which were bright and clean in 1975 had become shabby by the late eighties. Looking round the house now, I kept finding faults: that crack in the wall, the stains on the bedroom ceiling, the peeling wallpaper in the hall.

I decided to do something about this deterioration, starting with the downstairs bathroom, which was visibly suffering from damp. It wasn't an ideal bathroom and never would be: it had originally been a coal cellar and was small and windowless but there was no other room in the narrow Victorian house that could easily be converted. Some twelve years earlier we had removed the bath and had a shower installed. This solved the worst problem posed by the room in that you no longer banged your bum against the wall as you bent to pick up your towel. But now some of the tiles of the shower tray were coming out, revealing soggy wood underneath.

Having got two estimates for curing the damp and replacing the tiles, one alarmingly high and one suspiciously low, I had a discussion with my brother-in-law, to whom I turned for help with certain practical tasks which I found difficult (viz. all kinds of household repairs and anything to do with the car) and he advised me to accept the low estimate, provided the firm would give me a guarantee. 'You're paying for the gold leaf on the fucking brochure if you go with the other wankers,' was his comment on the better-known firm. The smaller, less expensive firm turned out to be one man who laughed too hard at his own jokes. He assured me that a ten-year guarantee would be issued as soon as the job was done, arrived the next day with a mate and based himself in the bathroom, gradually pushing outwards in what seemed like an attempt to take over the house.

He piled tins in the living room and planks in the hallway. He made free with the telephone, picking it up whenever it rang, ready for a chat with the caller, instead of allowing the answer machine to record messages.

'Your hubby rang from Tahiti,' he announced cheerfully, meeting me inside the front door as I arrived home from Birmingham. 'All right for some. When are you joining him?'

My heart lurched as I remembered the time that Paul and I had been together in Tahiti. We had slept in a palm-roofed cabin, ridden a motor scooter through the heat, visited the anthropologist Bengt Danielsson (Kon-Tiki veteran turned anti-nuclear lobbyist), swum underwater among luminous fish.

'Chance would be a fine thing,' I said, clutching at clichés. 'Some of us have to work for a living. How are you getting on with the tiles?'

'Couldn't start on that. Mick forgot the grout, didn't he?'

On another occasion he took a personal call of his own, unaware that the recording device had been activated; later I listened to a long conversation in which the person at the other end demanded money in an acrimonious tone, and my man sounded conciliatory and untrustworthy.

At least it was someone to come home to.

Monday 15th October

Hungover so couldn't go to Piers Paul Read's party after interviewing him about his novel, On the Third Day.

⌒

Not so much couldn't as didn't want to, I think. I liked Piers Paul Read, despite his uncompromising religious views, but I wasn't ready to be quizzed by him or other guests about Paul. The idea of talking to writers socially, outside the safe boundaries of an interview, raised another concern: what kind of place, if any, did I have in the literary world Paul and I had moved in as a couple? It overlapped at the edges with my world of journalism, but clearly there were inner circles to which I did not belong in any other guise than as Paul's wife. Much more important was the fact that it would be hard to remain sober at a publication party and I had resolved not to drink that evening, partly as a penance for having a glass too many the night before, and partly (this was crucial) to keep my head clear for the following day. The Booker Prize for Fiction was being awarded and I would be covering it in a live edition of *Meridian*.

Tuesday 16th October

Booker Meridian.

My job was to sit in the studio in London, explain what the Booker Prize was and then speak on a line to my colleague Christopher Cook. He would be at the Guildhall in his dinner jacket, schmoozing the literati, preparing to grab the winner after the announcement (scheduled for 8.45pm) and persuade her to say a few words before our programme ended at 9pm. We knew who the winner was; we had known for several hours, but were bound by solemn oaths to secrecy. The oaths really were solemn; if we broke the embargo we would be punished, blacklisted, no more dinner invitations, no more interviews with prize-winning authors. My fear was that as we went on air, a devil would enter me and prod me to blurt out the name.

It wasn't the first time I had experienced the Booker Prize award ceremony at a distance. In the seventies, when I first began producing a book programme for the World Service, my presenter bagged the one invitation we were sent and my only contact with the proceedings was to listen later to the tapes on which he had recorded bookish comments against a background of inebriated chatter. It was the year Paul Scott won for *Staying On* – the codicil to his *Raj Quartet*; he was too ill to attend the dinner and his daughter accepted the prize on his behalf. Philip Larkin, who was the chairman of the judges, made a gracious speech, defining the difference between poetry and prose. Much later, I read Larkin's account of the evening in a letter, in which he recalled in irreverent terms how some of those present, including himself, had been the worse for alcohol, confessing he felt terrible next day.* I liked the sound of Philip Larkin, though some people who have read his letters and authorised biography would take a different view. Mr Miseryguts, one reviewer called him.

I managed to attend the Booker award ceremony myself (but not, as I recall, the dinner) the year William Golding won the prize for *Fire Down Below*. My money was on his rival, Anthony Burgess, for *Earthly Powers* and I had recorded an interview with Burgess which was ready to broadcast. Golding had refused to be interviewed before the event. I joined the huddle of hacks holding out microphones, desperate to catch a

* Quoted in *Philip Larkin: A Writer's Life* by Andrew Motion.

few words. He said something, I don't remember what. Nothing about good and evil or whether human beings are intrinsically cruel. The book is about fellatio in the navy in the 18th century.

The following year, Paul was a judge and so I attended the dinner as a guest. Sitting next to me was the writer Hunter Davies, who was deploring my decision to remove my children from the state system of education and send them to a public school – 'It will screw them up completely' – when the chairman of the judges rose to announce that the prize had been awarded to a tiny, well-written and uncontentious novel about a Thames barge, by Penelope Fitzgerald. At the time it seemed an odd choice from a shortlist which included V.S. Naipaul and Patrick White. Paul told me that 'over my dead body' threats had blocked the major contenders. One judge had ruled out Naipaul's book, *A Bend in the River*, on the grounds that it was misogynistic.

Having once been a guest at the dinner, I was less inclined in subsequent years to vie with colleagues for the chance to attend professionally. Let others enjoy the privilege of staying sober while all around made merry; let others elbow through the highbrow throng to pounce on the winner. Over the past years, J.M. Coetzee, Nadine Gordimer, Iris Murdoch, Kingsley Amis and Salman Rushdie had won the prize.

'And the winner of the 1990 Booker Prize for Fiction,' the chairman of the judges revealed at 8.50pm, five minutes behind schedule (would Christopher have time to grab her?) 'is A.S. Byatt, for her novel *Possession*.'

As Antonia Byatt made her acceptance speech at the Guildhall, I discussed the book on air with Peter Kemp, while at the back of my mind danced private memories of the few occasions when the winner's path and mine had crossed – once quite literally on a family walk near Box Hill; at other times, less surprisingly, in recording studios: she was a regular reviewer for radio arts programmes. We also knew her sister, the novelist Margaret Drabble.

But we had first met in 1975. *The Great Railway Bazaar* had been published and acclaimed, Paul's breakthrough. My affair while he was away had almost wrecked our marriage, but we had decided to stay together and to move from our terraced house in Catford to a bigger one in a better area. We found the perfect home in Wandsworth: Victorian, double fronted, spacious with good-sized rooms, well laid out, backed by a long garden with herbaceous borders and ornaments from the set of Peter Brook's *Midsummer Night's Dream* (not included in the sale). There was a railway line at the bottom of the garden. The house belonged to Mr and Mrs Duffy.

'You're a writer, aren't you?' said Mrs Duffy to Paul, pausing on the landing, on our way to inspect the bedrooms. 'I am too. My pen name is A.S. Byatt.'

'Oh yes, of course,' we said, though I don't believe either of us had read her books then. I was nudging Paul to indicate that the house was just what I wanted.

'Let's offer the full price,' I said, as we drove back to Catford. I think it was £25,000. But the Duffys received a better offer, from someone who had ready cash. We would need a mortgage; that could take time. Mr Duffy rang to tell us. We refused to bargain. There was some acrimony. Eventually we bought another house in Wandsworth, which we liked almost as much. Many years later when I talked to Antonia Byatt at a

BBC party, she was apologetic and blamed the men. 'They felt they had to lock horns.'

'It doesn't matter,' I said. 'We found another nice house.'

She seemed relieved. We both had drinks in our hands. She talked a good deal about Balzac, who was her favourite writer ('I want to write books like Balzac,' she said. 'I don't want to write books like my sister') and I talked about malaria because I was making a programme about it for the African Service. 'I think Balzac would have been interested in malaria,' she offered, like an olive branch. I accepted it.

'And now,' I said, having heard on my headphones that Christopher had seized her as she left the podium, 'Christopher Cook is at the Guildhall ready to talk to A.S. Byatt, the winner of this year's Booker Prize.'

And on my programme, (*Meridian*, 16th October 1990) she told the world that she planned to build a swimming pool with the £20,000 she had won.

Wednesday 24th October

Took Hungarians to Cardiff.

⌒

Six Hungarians had arrived, their course overlapping with the Poles', so that for a hectic week there were a dozen Eastern Europeans for us to ferry around. Idalia, Paweł, Marek, Andrzej and Grażyna flew back to Poland on 27th October. (Lesław had been called back early to cover the elections.) Six more Poles would arrive next week. Applications from Czechoslovakia for a course in the New Year were piled high on the Head of Training's desk.

'It's too bloody much. I don't know how I'm going to get through all this,' she shouted, slamming the door of her office, rejecting offers of help.

Meanwhile I visited Louis in Oxford where he was sharing a house on Princes Street (between St Clements and the Cowley Road) with five other students, but not Susanna ('Not a good idea to live with your girlfriend,' he said). I also went to a Monet exhibition at the Academy with a friend who was visiting from New York.

'Why don't you come to the States for Christmas?' she said.

'?'

'Why don't you come to the States for Christmas?'

Of course. I had been wondering how to spend Christmas, my first without Paul. This was perfect. Marcel would be there on vacation from Yale, Louis and I could stay in a hotel, if Paul wanted to join us, that might be negotiated ... And my friend had a house in Sag Harbor where we could spend Christmas Day. It would be a good way to end one year and start the next.

Now I was able to look forward to Christmas with pleasure, other things became clear. At the beginning of January I would return to England for the second three months of my contract with BBC Training, deciding at that point whether I wanted to extend it further. VSO would be letting me know about overseas postings and if I were offered a job somewhere interesting, I would take that up when the BBC contract ended. The last months had proved that working full-time felt safer than the ups and downs of freelancing. It seemed to be doing me good.

Monday 29th October

Made provisional booking to go to N.Y.

⌒

The next day the Head of Training called me into her office.

'Sit down love.' She swung her legs onto her desk.

'I'm not going to be able to get the Czech course off the ground until April.'

The plan had been that the first group of Czechs would arrive in February and I would run the course before my contract ended in March. Presumably she was now going to ask me to extend my contract. I would probably say yes. If there was a clash with the VSO posting, I could sort it out later.

'So I really can't justify keeping you on after Christmas.'

I said nothing. She had felled me. Then she held out a hand.

'Not full-time that is. But I can offer you three days a week – to help with setting up. Maybe in some ways it will suit you better,' she said meaningfully. 'You know, give you more time for your other work.'

I knew she suspected me of pursuing my other work in her time, slipping out of the office to do interviews. Her suspicions were unfounded.

'It's rather short notice. I've already turned down freelance work.'

'I think you'll find the contract says a month. Anyway, think about whether you want the three days a week or not and let me know.'

Later, I looked at the small print on my contract. She was right: it could be terminated by either side with a month's warning. So I was to be booted out of my job in Training now; what ignominy! I wanted to tell her to stuff her three days a week but decided to wait until I felt calmer.

That evening I opened another letter from my postings officer at VSO. She still hadn't found me a job. She sounded doubtful that she would.

Two reversals, after two good months. What would the next one be? Slings and arrows. How could I ward them off?

Wednesday 31st October

After work attended Insight Seminar at Mount Royal Hotel near Marble Arch.

Chapter 13

November

Thursday 1st November

Insight.

～

I had signed up for a personal development seminar spread over several evenings and a weekend. Tonight's session was about effectiveness: 'How to get more of life's payoffs.' I was determined to put the lessons into practice. I'd been struggling all year. Where were my payoffs?

2nd November 1990

Postings Officer
Voluntary Service Overseas

Dear Maria,

Thank you for your letter. I was disappointed that the prospects of a VSO posting seem dim. Did nothing come of your hawking my CV? At a time when the importance of radio in development is so obvious, it's hard to believe that none of the countries you operate in wants a volunteer with my experience and qualifications.

I do hope you will continue to try to find a post. I feel that eventually something must come of it; but it is taking much longer than I expected when I applied nearly a year ago.

Saturday 3rd November

All day at Insight.

～

This session was about 'how to get rid of pain, or use it as feedback, to produce greater health'. Good advice, but I could see no obvious way of putting it into practice immediately. The young woman leading the session talked about how she had moved on from one failed relationship and made a better one. The whole process had taken several weeks, she said. Weeks? I'd been trying to move on for months.

Insight isn't as cranky as you might think (though Louis, an expert on weird cults, once told me it has an extra-terrestrial dimension; if this is true, I certainly wasn't aware of it). It was first promoted in Britain by Arianna Stassinopoulos (now Arianna Huffington) and Bernard Levin. Paul and I were invited to a launch party at the Café Royal in Regent Street and Paul got a big laugh and round of applause by asking hostile, ridiculing questions. I joined in the laughter and yet I secretly hankered for what was being offered. I mean, who would not want to 'connect to the natural ability each of us possesses to be joyful, loving and effective'? Who would not want to 'let go of the old limitations that have held you back and begin to experience your own uniqueness'? Who would not want to live their life in a 'higher, more fulfilling state'? You can say these phrases in a silly voice and laugh at them – but would you really pass up the chance?

At that time, in the seventies, I was searching elsewhere, in Buddhism, Sufism, the Gnostic Gospels and the work of G.I. Gurdjieff and I didn't pursue Insight. I practised Transcendental Meditation for a while, but had doubts when I heard that its devotees were learning to fly. When it comes to crankiness, we all draw the line somewhere. For similar, though not identical reasons, I had reservations about Bhagwan Shri

Rajneesh, though I knew people who were transformed by his teaching, appearing with new names and orange clothes. A little yoga and eclectic reading seemed enough to keep my spiritual flame alight. But when Paul left, I needed every prop available. Insight was recommended to me again by a friend. 'Don't they shout at you and stop you going to the toilet?' I asked. 'No, not at all. That's EST. This is much more benign. It's like taking exercise to make you fit,' he said.

So in much the same spirit as I'd visited a health farm the previous year, I joined a hundred other people who wanted to be fitter at the Mount Royal Hotel near Marble Arch. We would spend four evenings and two whole days together. On the first night, a tall, sun-tanned, one-armed Californian called Razz explained the rules. One was confidentiality – which I have in mind even as I write. Another was no drugs or alcohol, not even when we got home in the evenings; this alone would be beneficial. A third was punctuality: before every session we were to wait in the antechamber, two minutes before the start-time taped music would be played, the moment the music ended we must be in our seats. The music was Grieg's 'In the Hall of the Mountain King'. Its insistent sound haunts me now, a warning not to break the rules. *Didi didi didi dum* …

A few jottings will give an idea of my experience of Insight, without breaching confidentiality. *Didi dum dum*:

1. The Game of Life
The first evening we were divided into two teams and sent to separate rooms to prepare for a game. We were told the aim was to achieve the highest possible score. (Never mind how, that isn't important.) The team I was in pressed on, in a very

competitive way, cheering when our opponents lost a round (What the hell were they up to? They seemed to be throwing it away!), cock-a-hoop when our final score was much higher than theirs. We had trounced them! Razz then revealed that the 'highest possible score' referred to the aggregate score of the two teams. We hadn't won. We had completely missed the point. N.B. Apply to life. To marriage?

2. Giving and Receiving Positive and Negative Feedback

You had to go up to someone in the room whom you liked and tell them why, using a carefully structured formula. It began: 'The inner beauty I perceive in you is ...' I said it to a vulnerable-looking woman who, in a previous exercise, had admitted feeling lost and alone. Several other people chose her too; is vulnerability attractive? No one came up to me. No one had perceived my inner beauty. Perhaps I didn't have any. But then I wasn't approached in the next exercise either, which was telling someone, frankly but tactfully, what you didn't like about them. I converged with a number of others on a small man who had been bumptious and obnoxious from the start.

'Tom, the way you hide your inner beauty from me, is by always trying to dominate other people and never listening to what they say ...' Tom took it on the chin, making the correct response: 'Thank you for caring enough to share that with me.' The fourth time he said the words they rang hollow and his mouth twitched.

3. Sharing

Two or three times a day a microphone was passed round and people volunteered to talk into it, telling the rest of us what they were feeling. To show the way, Razz described how he had felt when his arm was torn off by a speedboat, not the immediate physical pain (indescribable and unimaginable) but waking up in hospital to realise he could no longer surf, swim and play basketball – or so he thought; later he learnt to do all these things superbly well, despite his handicap. An African man revealed in a low voice that his wife had left him for someone else. Several people said they felt lonely and unloved. Several people wept. One woman asked for money. Razz talked gently to those who were most distressed, inviting them to look for hope beyond their pain. Then an angry man snatched the microphone and told Razz he was a shyster, exploiting people, it was disgusting. Razz's benign expression changed and he took a very different tack, beginning 'Now see here ...,' and ending 'and if you don't like it, you can just walk right out that door, buddy.' The man fell silent but did not leave.

Sunday 4th November
Insight. Shared.

Well, it was almost the last day so I felt I had to put up my hand and take the microphone. Be a sport. Be one of the gang. It's something I've always found hard. So I just talked about how nervous I felt, and how this was odd, since I was, after all, a broadcaster and used to talking into microphones. The others applauded politely, kindly. What I said was sincere. But I said nothing about my broken marriage and my broken heart. That pain couldn't be shared. Not with a hundred strangers in a hall.

Not even with my family or friends. Perhaps not fully with myself. It was still too distressing, too confusing.

Sometimes I walked steadily towards the future, thinking, yes, I'm doing well; then a dark pit would gape open in front of me and it took all my strength not to fall in. The seminar reminded me that other people looked into dark pits too, though I wasn't sure if what was in them was the same.

Insight did not, in the end, become my way of understanding what was in the pit. But despite sceptical reservations, I did feel better at the end of the seminar and I made a good friend there.

Back at the office, I accepted the offer of working in Training three days a week after Christmas. It would provide an element of regular work and leave time for the draining task of deciding what I really wanted to do with my life.

Monday 5th November

Collected new group of Poles from St Giles and brought them to Bush.

The Hungarians were touring Britain with Klara; my second group of Poles had just arrived. The course was familiar now and I was mostly left to run it by myself, which I enjoyed.

Wednesday 7th November

Gave Death on the Rock *lecture and chaired other sessions.*

Took Poles to Parliament to talk to Peter Bottomley and Tony Worthington.

Attended debate. Tony Benn talked about the Gulf.

⟡

The two MPs patiently explained how the British parliamentary system worked, then showed us the way to the public gallery. The last time I had sat there was nearly 30 years earlier, just after I'd taken my O levels, when my form teacher had decided to fill the dead time between the end of exams and the start of the summer holidays with educational trips to acquaint us with the institutions of democracy: Parliament, the Law Courts, the Town Hall. It was the summer of 1959, I was sixteen, the debate in the Commons was about the death of eleven prisoners in Hola detention camp in Kenya. They had been beaten by the guards because they refused to perform manual labour. The prison authorities had lied and said they died from drinking contaminated water. I was shocked. My cursory newspaper reading (mostly my mother's *Daily Express*) had made me aware that members of a cult called Mau Mau had committed atrocities in Kenya and taken oaths solemnised by bestial rites. Now I heard another version, in which people claiming self-government were brutally suppressed. This version had an unmistakable ring of truth. It has been said that the deaths in Hola camp and public outrage at the crime sped up the release of Jomo Kenyatta from prison and the granting of independence to Kenya: *Uhuru* was celebrated four years later in 1963. Two years after that, I arrived in Nairobi with a dozen other VSOs. On the anniversary of independence I attended a parade and a ball. Jomo Kenyatta waved his fly whisk at me.

Today's debate was also disturbing. Tony Benn warned of the consequences of making war on Iraq. It would be a dangerous act of aggression. It would be wrong. He spoke with passionate conviction, but this time I couldn't feel the certainty of moral outrage. American and British troops were gathering in their thousands in Saudi Arabia because Saddam Hussein had invaded Kuwait in August. Newspapers reported atrocities: in Kuwaiti hospitals, babies had been snatched from incubators by Iraqi troops. Hostages had been taken. Saddam Hussein was a cruel tyrant. I didn't know if Tony Benn was right or wrong.

I stayed in my seat long after the Poles had made polite excuses and slipped away. They were bored. The only British politician they were interested in was Mrs Thatcher and she had left the Commons by the time we arrived. Earlier in the day she had said: 'Time is running out for Saddam Hussein. Either he gets out of Kuwait soon or we and our allies will remove him by force.' But time was running out for her too. A few days earlier, Sir Geoffrey Howe had resigned from the Cabinet and delivered a devastating attack on her leadership.

Friday 9th November

Interviewed Ali Mazrui.

Ali Mazrui had just published a book of essays called *Cultural Forces in World Politics*. As a professor at Makerere University, Kampala, in the sixties, he had given a lecture to the group of trainee teachers to which I belonged and impressed me with a brave criticism of the Kenyan government's anti-Asian policies. (At that time the Kenyans, newly independent under Jomo Kenyatta, discriminated against their Asian citizens more than the Ugandans under Milton Obote did; this changed a few years later when Idi Amin came to power in Uganda and expelled all the Asians from the country, making them stateless.) Mazrui's lecture was in the same series as Paul's 'Tarzan is an Expatriate', my first sight of him. They both published their lectures in *Transition* magazine, which was edited by Rajat Neogy. Since then, Mazrui had held professorships at various universities in America, presented a series called *The Africans* on British television and given the Reith lectures.

We talked for some time in the studio about East Africa and the people we had known there, especially Rajat Neogy, the charismatic Ugandan Asian whose career path had spiralled downwards as spectacularly as Ali Mazrui's had ascended. Rajat's magazine, *Transition*, was considered seditious because it criticised the government of Uganda and Rajat had been imprisoned by Obote, then released and expelled from the country. He and his family moved to Ghana and Rajat ran the magazine from Accra, but his spirit had been broken. He started drinking heavily and having visions. He converted to Islam. The last I'd heard was that he was in California, impoverished. His former wife, Barbara, lived in New York and I told Mazrui that I hoped to see her when I went there at Christmas.

'And Paul? I've followed his career. What's he doing now?'

'He's travelling in the Pacific.'

'Remember me to him.'

'Certainly. He's an admirer of your work.' Was that true? Paul had once satirised Mazrui's referential prose style in an article by-lined *A. Mzuri*.

'As I am of his.'

We shook hands and I asked him to sign my copy of his book. This wasn't something I usually did, but the thought occurred to me that I might not see him again.

Tuesday 20th November

Result of Tory leadership election.

Michael Heseltine stood against Mrs Thatcher in the first round of the election (having previously said he would never challenge her) and secured 152 votes – enough to ensure that there would be a second round in which others would close in for the kill. Television viewers (I was one) watched Mrs Thatcher burst out of a meeting in the Paris Embassy, and bear down on a commentator who was hunched over his microphone, speculating that at this point she would withdraw from the contest. 'She's behind you!' we shouted at our screens, until at last, taking the man by surprise, she commandeered the microphone and announced that she had every intention of standing again and winning.

Went to visit Yvette and swapped views on unfaithful husbands.

Yvette was the friend I made at the Insight seminar. We were drawn to each other because our stories touched and matched at certain points.

She was French, married to an English businessman who had become wealthy and successful during the years of the marriage. (When they met they were both students.) They had a daughter. In the last few years, their marriage had deteriorated, though Yvette didn't know why: they quarrelled, he sulked, they didn't enjoy being together anymore and eventually she was provoked to tell her husband to leave. He packed his clothes, called a taxi and went to live with another woman, a colleague from work, with whom he had been having an affair for years. Yvette hadn't known, though she had been introduced to the woman by her husband and had even entertained her in the family home.

'My husband had an affair too,' I confided. 'But he said it wasn't important. He said he could easily have given her up. That wasn't the reason he left.'

In the manner we had learned at the Insight seminar, we prepared affirmations – short sentences we would say to ourselves when our confidence was flagging (I don't think I'll give examples; they sound silly) and we made resolutions for the future about finding new friends, being more open, taking more risks. We decided that Yvette would put an advertisement in the lonely hearts column of *Time Out* and I would look for a new house.

Thursday 22nd November

Went to Nottingham.
    Thatcher resigned!

I was escorting the new group of Poles round radio and television stations in Nottingham when we heard the news. In the last two days Margaret Thatcher must have realised that to struggle on would mean humiliation. This way she left undefeated, head high, with only a trace of self-pity in the comment with which she summed up her betrayal: 'It's a funny old world.'

Her resignation meant our visits to broadcasting stations were enlivened by an excited flurry of speculation: 'This John Major's a bit of a dark horse.' 'Well of course I interviewed him way back, when he was at the DHSS.' 'He used to be a Lambeth councillor.' 'Thank God she's gone.'

The Poles were bemused by the fall of their heroine.

Saturday 24th November

Drove to North London to check out houses.

⌒

Was moving the answer?

My bathroom was finished and looked fine, though I was still pursuing the ten-year guarantee I had been promised: the last time I tried to call my man, his phone had been disconnected. But when I looked round the house to see what more needed doing, there was so much – too much perhaps.

I saw an advertisement featuring converted warehouses in North East London and drove over there to look. The apartments were not yet completed and it was hard to imagine what they would be like. Where would the living room be? Where would I sleep? It was impossible to envisage my life in that strange part of London, in that odd, empty, unfinished shell, half torn down, half rebuilt. What sort of life would it be? Who would I share it with? Driving home, listening to tapes in the car – John Denver, *Carmen* and highlights of *Tristan and Isolde* – I felt disturbed and nearly caused a crash during the

'Liebestod'. I apologised to the angry motorist whom I had cut off and continued my journey, muttering Insight affirmations about being a unique, loving and loveable person.

November 27th 1990

Dear Mum and Dad

I am looking forward very much to our pre-Christmas celebration. I am also looking forward to being in New York with Marcel and Louis over Christmas.

Enclosed is a copy of a letter I wrote to Paul's mother a month ago which I think says what I feel. Perhaps I am even more certain now that I must put the past behind me and make a future on my own. And it won't be a bad one either. I have all sorts of ideas about what I want to do.

I really appreciate your support over the past months, which have been difficult, but I do see light at the end of the tunnel and am much more confident about my ability to survive and be happy than I was six months ago. Rosamond has also been a great help and support to me.

Don't worry about what to tell the relatives. I will enclose a suitable note with my Christmas cards. Refer them to me if they ask you any questions.

I look forward to 1991 with optimism and confidence. It will be different but it will be good.

The last sentence sounds like another affirmation. If only it were as simple as that! My parents thanked me for the letter when we next spoke on the phone but we didn't discuss it. Some years later, when I was going through my mother's effects, I found it tucked away in her dressing table drawer in an envelope with my name on.

The letter I had written to Paul's mother explained that I loved Paul but felt I couldn't continue in the marriage without a firm commitment from him. It was a good, straight letter and writing it made me seem a better person than the one who had screamed and called him a bastard. Was that hypocritical? I did mean what I wrote, especially when I told her I didn't want to lose touch and that I would never regret the marriage. The note of resignation was premature, in the letters to both sets of parents. Like Margaret Thatcher, I was reluctant to go.

But she had eventually thrown in the towel. Now John Major was Prime Minister. Within days, this would no longer be surprising or strange.

Wednesday 28th November

Took Poles (Jacek, Piotr and Maria) to Glasgow. Drinks as usual with Jack Regan.

Thursday 29th November

Dropped the Poles at the BBC then went to the Burrell Collection.

The familiar trip to Scotland: too much whisky and Scottish nationalism the first night, then visits to the BBC newsroom, Scottish Television and Radio Clyde. At least the Burrell Collection was a pleasant surprise, both the objects in it and its setting.

As I walked through Pollok Park on that clear autumnal day (November was fine, not damp and drizzly), I remembered it was Thanksgiving in America and wondered what Paul was doing. Sitting with his family, round the table, I supposed. Or would be in a few hours' time. In the 22 years we had been married, I had never been in the United States for Thanksgiving. But then I had never lived in America, only spent holidays there. Resentment made me pick up speed and hunch my shoulders. Through me, Paul had entered British life and inhabited it, before he eventually decided he didn't like this country. He had done the things that British people do: paid taxes (grudgingly), owned property, had a mortgage and a library ticket, watched Coronation Street, gone to dog races, Glyndebourne and Guy Fawkes parties. The arrangement hadn't been reciprocal. The United States had not been opened up for me in the same way. I had never celebrated Thanksgiving there, or July 4th, or seen a New England fall, though I did have a multiple entry visa in my passport and two children with dual nationality.

'I haven't made the most of it,' I thought, circumambulating the lawn for the second time, with my hands in my pockets. It had been my choice as well as Paul's to base ourselves in Britain all these years, but I had always imagined that one day, preferably not too soon, we would live properly in America and invite his family for Thanksgiving dinner. (I had learned to make pumpkin pie from a colleague in Singapore.)

The trees were almost bare. It was winter now. Paul would be lighting a fire. The guests would be on their way. I wanted to be there too.

Was it too late?

Chapter 14

December

Sunday 2nd December

Tidying Louis' room found letter which upset me greatly.

～

The reward for attempting to clear up Louis' messy room was occasional glimpses of his secret world. Once on his pinboard I found a large splinter, sellotaped to a piece of paper, with a carefully written note, like a label in a museum: *This splinter was under my thumbnail from June 3rd to June 21st 1980.* Another time I discovered an orange exercise book from Tower House School (*In Bono Vince*), the prep school we sent him to when he was nine. He hated it. Written across the book in red ink were the words TOP SECRET. Despite the warning, I opened the book: many years had passed, it was permissible. Inside was a list of teachers' names with defining comments:

> *Mr F: teaches scripture, music and Latin to Form II. Lashes out suddenly. Hits and gives lines.*
> *Mr P: teaches English to Forms I & II. Tattletales. A bad teacher. Gives lines but forgets.*

There was also a list of the boys in his class, again with comments:

> *This boy is tortured and persecuted. (Picks his nose.)*
> *This boy could not spell his own name.*

Louis was twenty now. On the top of the desk was a letter, out of its envelope, half hidden underneath a book on madness by Michel Foucault. I straightened the book and saw that the letter was from Marcel. I unfolded it. It had been written and sent earlier in the year.

The letter was in the form of a short story – a Chandleresque third-person narrative, featuring a cool sleuth called Raymond Marseille (Marcel himself; his second name is Raymond) and someone called the Old Man, who was clearly Paul. Raymond Marseille finds traces of a female visitor in his father's house: a hairdryer in the bedroom, a chocolate yoghurt in the fridge. Then he discovers some photos: the Old Man with a dark-haired woman coming out of a restaurant in Honolulu; the Old Man and the same woman, dressed for skiing, in Vermont. One evening Raymond is having dinner with the Old Man and the phone rings. 'I can't talk now,' the Old Man mutters furtively into the receiver. Half an hour later the fax machine beeps and whirrs, spilling out a love fax, from Honolulu. This was transcribed word for word, including the name and address of the woman who sent it. It included phrases like 'I love you; I adore you. I can't get used to sleeping alone,' and, most hurtfully, reminders of times spent together, including words and gestures which I recognised as Paul's. Hidden in that fax within a story in a letter, lay the truth, like a murder weapon.

I sat on the floor and hugged my knees. My heart banged against them. My Insight strength drained away as I pieced together the clues Raymond Marseille had provided. It wasn't difficult. Last January after leaving me, Paul had fled straight to this woman in Hawaii. Then she had accompanied him to our house on Cape Cod. They had gone skiing together at the place where we had skied as a family the previous year.

Hadn't I known something like this was happening? Yes, I suppose so, but I had pretended not to. When it was spelt out with a name and address and details like a hairdryer and choco-late yoghurt, it was no longer possible to pretend.

How could he? And at the same time say he loved me still? The phrase 'It's a funny old world' tolled in my mind. Self-pity engulfed me, then a wave of anger on behalf of our sons. Anger and shame. They had been made the keepers of unwelcome secrets. They had forfeited the open relationship with their parents which was their right.

Marcel hadn't known what to do with the knowledge forced upon him. He had tried to turn it into fiction, distancing himself by writing in the third person. Then he had sent it to his brother, needing to share the bitter secret. Louis had left it on his desk. Both of them had wanted me to read it. They wanted to end our complicit deception.

I rang Paul and got his answerphone so I repeated the name of the woman several times in a crazy kind of way and hung up. Later he rang me back.

'Why did you leave the name of a woman on my answerphone?'

'I think we need to start being honest. This isn't fair on the kids.'

'I do know somebody of that name. But not very well. She isn't important.'

I told him about the story.

'You shouldn't have read it. You've got the wrong idea.'

Was that possible?

'What wrong idea?'

'She isn't important.'

Can someone who flies thousands of miles to ski with you and sleep with you, and tells you she adores you, not be important?

Perhaps. My head hurt. I didn't know.

Friday 7th December

Can't remember.

⁓

Philip Larkin wrote a poem about keeping a diary called 'Forget What Did'.* It suggests that abandoning a diary leaves you free to remember the essentials, not the facts. I was looking forward to abandoning mine soon, on 31st December, less than three weeks' away. I didn't enjoy writing it; why had I kept it up for so long? It was, I think, an attempt to pin down the truth when it was slipping about in a way that might drive me mad. An attempt which hadn't been entirely successful.

At least a diary is more reliable than literature, where truth conflicts with art. Larkin wrote about that too, in a letter to a woman who had shown him the manuscript of a novel about the death of her son. '*I can quite see that to "play about" with the kind of subject matter you have taken would seem heartless, frivolous, even untrue, an offence against decency and decent feelings, something you couldn't do, and yet in literature it somehow has to be done – one might almost say that it's the mixture of truth and untruth that makes literature.*'†

Lao Tzu puts it more bluntly: '*True words are not fine-sounding; fine-sounding words are not true.*'

'Can't remember' is an honest diary entry in its way, acknowledging that there are omissions in my account of the year. Why is there no mention of some of my most important friends? Because I didn't talk to them, or because a conversation

* Larkin's *Collected Poems*.
† Letter quoted in *Philip Larkin: A Writer's Life* by Andrew Motion.

with a friend may be as unremarkable as putting on a pair of old slippers?

There was one event not recorded in the diary which I know occurred in December 1990. Later it assumed a significance it didn't have at the time. It was an evening spent in the BBC Club with a friend and colleague.

I had bumped into his wife in June, at the Open Day in central London for people interested in becoming couple counsellors and I had assumed that, like me, she was there because her own marriage was in trouble. Later a mutual friend confirmed that this was so, that her husband had left her for another woman. Now I heard his account.

Yes, he had left his wife to live with another woman. It was a romantic passion which ignited when his wife took a job abroad for six months, leaving him alone in London. The other woman was an art historian, an expert on Renaissance patronage. He loved her; he also loved his wife.

For two years they had tried an arrangement by which he lived with the other woman from Monday to Thursday and his wife from Friday to Sunday. This was convenient because it meant he and his wife could still go to dinner parties as if they were a 'normal' married couple, but in every other way it was a bad solution, causing jealousy, pain and misery. His wife eventually called a halt. He must choose. He chose her; of course he did, as well as fifteen years of shared memories, his hard-earned savings were invested in the marriage, in the house they had fixed up together. He chose his wife and the house and then cheated, slipping out to meet his lover. He was caught and the choice was presented again. He left his wife. He was living with the other woman in a tiny flat not far from my house in Wandsworth.

'You must come for a meal,' he said.

'I'm about to go to America. Maybe in the New Year.'

He drove me home and (this is what confirms the date) I saw that the light was on in Louis' bedroom. He was home from Oxford for the holiday. I rushed into the house, eager to see Louis, not looking back.

With hindsight, as I say, that evening was important. That man became part of my life. At the time, since I forgot to enter it in the diary, presumably it seemed less significant than visits with the Poles to TV Centre, Sky Television, *The Times*, the Jimmy Young Show, the parties I went to in the run-up to Christmas, the books I read, the plays I saw.

Friday 14th December

Last day of last Polish course.

Went with Louis and Susanna to see Racing Demon *at The National.*

∾

Then in different colour ink – which may simply mean I added it later: *VSO, it seems, may have a job in Ghana, in May.*

A glimmer of hope or yet another mirage? Subsequent entries conjure memories of optimism.

Saturday 15th December

Insight party.

∾

The invitation said: *Dress – Fantastic!* So I wore a tight black skirt, fishnet stockings and strapless top. I stared at myself in the mirror and for once I liked the way I looked; pining away to skinniness had its advantages.

Sunday 16th December

The Worgans, Mum, Dad and Susanna came for lunch: salmon en croute.

Trying new recipes is always a sign of hope. This one worked well. My family ate hungrily and I was pleased. It was nearly Christmas. I was going to America. Then my mood changed yet again.

Tuesday 18th December

Letter from Alex.

Alex was my brother-in-law. His letter provided further and more recent information about the woman who was replacing me in Paul's life. It also deepened a family rift and eventually forced me to realise that losing Paul would mean I lost his family too. Without them, my life would be diminished. My American in-laws, with their French and Italian ancestry, had welcomed me into territory beyond my own family's horizons. Besides, I loved them all, especially Alex.

The first time I met Paul's family was in Medford, Massachusetts at the end of December 1967. It was my first visit to America, a few weeks after our Kampala wedding. I was nervous.

We had flown first to London. There was a wedding reception at our house in Streatham (was it still *my* house?), with canapés provided by a neighbour. My father made a speech and rowdy relatives from my mother's side of the family barracked him. Paul was charming; my parents were proud. They didn't appear to mind that our marriage in the Kampala registry office had been so different from their own exchange of vows at a Baptist church in Balham in 1932.

My mother, the eldest daughter in a harum-scarum family, had found security by falling in love with an honourable, sensible man, of whom she was always in awe. Having captivated him, against his better judgement, with her prettiness and gaiety (she loved clothes, dancing, games and jokes) she attempted to conform to his requirements and became an anxious housewife, fretting about what the neighbours would think if she didn't polish the brass front doorstep every day. Watching her on her hands and knees at this task, I resolved early in life not to be like her.

On the morning that Paul and I were due to leave London and fly to the States, she was busy in the kitchen, moving from cupboard to cupboard, shifting things in what seemed to me a particularly futile way. I was sitting at the table with a cup of coffee, wishing I could talk to her properly. Our relationship had become stormy when I was an adolescent and never fully recovered, but I loved her. Without turning round, she said, in an angry, breathless way, 'Of course it's fairly obvious you're going to have a baby.'

I gulped a mouthful of coffee. 'Oh, you know. Does it show already?'

'I saw the slacks in the wardrobe.' I had bought a pair of trousers with an expanding waistband.

'I was going to tell you anyway. I hope you're pleased. We are.'

'Your father and I are so ashamed we can hardly sleep.'

There wasn't much to say after that. I wept for most of my first transatlantic flight. Paul's family were Catholics. His mother was very religious. What would she think of me?

It was almost a relief when an hour before we were due to land, the pilot announced that because of heavy snow in the Boston area, we would be diverted to Detroit. My first night in the United States of America was spent at a hotel in a city I have never visited since and which I didn't see at the time because of the dark and snow. From our luxurious time-capsule we rang Paul's home in Massachusetts. His parents, brothers and sisters came to the phone one by one and greeted me with voices that would become familiar.

'Hi Anne. Welcome to America!'

The next day the snow had stopped. We stood in the hotel lobby waiting for the shuttle bus to take us back to the airport. Next to me was a man holding a covered, bell-shaped object from which another American voice squawked: 'Hello. Hello. How do you do?'

Paul and I looked at each other and at the man, who lifted the cloth, saying, 'It's a mynah bird.'

'Hello, hello. How do you do?'

I was aware of the life fluttering inside me. My own hidden creature waiting to greet the world.

'You'd better tell her as soon as we get there,' I said, on the flight from Detroit to Boston.

His father met us at the airport and drove us to the house in Medford where the whole family, except Gene, the eldest brother, was waiting ... hugging us, exclaiming, gathering round the table in the big, warm kitchen, eating lasagne, ice cream and chocolate chip cookies, talking constantly, interrupting, laughing.

The picture in my mind is in perpetual motion. People get up to fetch more food, bring piles of plates to the sink, find a book, a school report, a letter, return to sit in different places, always talking. Paul's father is at one end of the table. He has a French face: high cheekbones, hooked nose, brown eyes like Paul's, behind rimless glasses. When he speaks, which is less frequently than anyone else, there is a clipped, harsh quality to his voice. 'Why doncha getcha hair cut?' he remarks to Paul and Alex. He becomes animated on the subject of the Battle of Bunker Hill.

'Those Redcoats didn't know what hit them.' He speaks as if it happened yesterday. 'Do they teach you about that in England?'

'Al loves history,' Paul's mother interrupts from the other end of the table. 'I do too. I'm doing a project with my class on the War of Independence. Have a doughnut, dear. Do you have doughnuts in England?'

And clustered round the table, though I couldn't say in exactly what order, are Peter, a cute ten year old, Joseph, a brooding adolescent, Mary, sixteen, smiling, with long brown hair, Ann Marie, almost my age, a teacher like her mother and engaged to be married, Paul, sitting next to me with his arm around my shoulders protectively and Alex, eighteen months older than Paul, tall, dark and dressed in black.

Paul had told me more about Alex than about anyone else in the family. He had spent two years in a Trappist monastery. He was doing a PhD on Samuel Beckett. Women fell desperately in love with him. He had a cloak and a sword. And here he was, doing imitations, telling stories, raising his arms to conduct: 'All together now.'

And they sang, 'Has Paul brought us any presents?' to the tune of 'We wish you a Merry Christmas'. Paul distributed knick-knacks we had bought in Africa.

'Paul tells me you're going to have a baby!'

It was the next day and Paul's mother and I were sharing some domestic task – was I cutting cookies or chopping onions for a spaghetti sauce – or possibly admiring the stained glass decorations she had made at craft class? Whatever implement I held went limp in my hand.

'Yes. It's a bit soon.'

She sighed and smiled and continued with what she was doing. 'That's love.'

We worked together in silence for a moment or two.

'Where will you have the baby?'

'There's a very good hospital in Kampala. It's called Mulago.'

'Will they give you pain relief?'

'I don't know. Will it hurt?'

She hesitated, searching for words.

'Medication is helpful. I didn't have any when Peter was born because it all happened too fast, but …'. She told me in some detail about her experiences of childbirth.

'I think of it as the Valley of the Shadow of Death.'

This made me think of my own mother's story of her first confinement. It had lasted a long time and she became aware from the behaviour of the medical staff, that something was wrong. Reaching down, she touched a tiny leg. 'Don't do that!' said someone sharply and then she lost consciousness. When she woke up and asked for her baby she was told he was dead.

By contrast, her account of my own birth was comic. During the contractions she had greedily gasped gas and air, knocked herself out for a few seconds, opened her eyes and asked, 'Is it all over?'

'You'll be lucky!' The nurses jeered.

'You buggers!' she spat at them (it wasn't a word she normally used) and they laughed all the more.

'They were rough types,' said my mother, as if that justified her own linguistic lapse. 'The strange thing was that from the moment you were born, I completely forgot the pain. It was the happiest day of my life.'

Right now, though, I was upset by my mother's disapproval of my pregnancy, whereas Paul's mother seemed kind and understanding, as only other people's mothers can, and admirable in every way, with her seven children, her teaching job, her chocolate-chip cookies and her stained-glass pixies under mushrooms. A month earlier, on 4th December 1967, my name had become Anne Theroux, the same as hers. Before that, I had been Anne Castle.

'I'm sorry my mother's such a pain about her *craftwork*.' Paul said the word with an exaggerated American accent.

'No, no. She's really nice.' I meant it. Paul made a face.

Marcel once reminded me of a theme in Chaucer's *Canterbury Tales* – the battle for '*maistrye*' between men and women.

'Who had *maistrye* in Dad's family?' he quizzed me.

'Well, Dad's mother I suppose. She played the traditional role but she definitely ruled the roost.'

'And in your family?'

'My father.' There could be no doubt about that. I pictured my mother, crouched before the doorstep, rag and cleaning fluid at the ready, while my father stepped out briskly down the street, holding a briefcase.

'Exactly.' He was being annoyingly smug.

'So who had it out of me and your Dad?'

'That was the problem. You both wanted it.' He added that he hoped he would have *maistrye*, if and when he got married.

'What about an equal partnership?'

'Difficult.'

But at the end of December 1967, Marcel was still in his covered cage, and referred to as Sebastian. 'Watch out for arrows,' said Ann Marie and I had my first doubt about the name we had chosen.

Paul's sisters displayed effortlessly the feminine virtues I had not so far acquired. They were quick to clear the plates from the table, sweep the floor, wipe a stain from a work surface or laugh at their brothers' jokes. They appeared to do these things with pleasure.

'Philly supports Women's Lib,' Ann Marie told me. 'You don't, do you?'

'I'm not sure,' I prevaricated. Philly was the wife of Paul's oldest brother, Gene. They lived in Washington and we were going there to visit them.

Did I support Women's Lib, as it was called in the sixties? In theory, yes, but with no sense of personal urgency. So far in my life I hadn't noticed many disadvantages in being a girl. There were no brothers to receive preferential treatment, to be excused from household chores, allowed to show off, given better education and more food. At school I chose Latin instead of needlework, ancient history instead of cookery. My father approved these choices; my mother had little to say on the matter. She had left school at fifteen to take a job as a sales assistant in the lingerie department of Harvey Nichols. Once or twice she suggested that a woman's greatest happiness came through marriage and children. Seeing her on her knees, I found that hard to believe.

I went to university, as my father expected, (not something either of my parents had done) and then to Africa. By then, I was off my parents' map. What would I be? Something wonderful. They didn't know what and neither did I, but in Africa I might find out. That's what I had been trying to do when I met Paul.

Now I was four months pregnant and married to the most delightful and ambitious man in the world. For the first time I sensed with foreboding a conflict of interests that had something to do with gender. Could I be a good wife and also do something that would make my parents proud? I was on the lookout for examples.

Gene and Philly had just adopted a baby and there were dirty nappies and bottles in unexpected places in their Washington house. The baby slept much of the day and cried at night. Gene was harassed, Philly looked exhausted.

'I feel as though my life has ended,' she complained, leaning back on a vomit-stained sofa while Gene prepared a rudimentary meal. Philly had been a lawyer, like Gene, but had given up her job when the adoption agency offered them a child. Required now to stay at home, she said she was trying to be a writer, so far without success.

'I think I may be the greatest unpublished writer in the world!' she mumbled. She had a safety pin in her mouth and the baby on her lap with his bum exposed.

'Never play with art,' Paul warned her. 'That's what Naipaul says.'

'That's so sententious,' mocked Alex, who had joined us in Washington and was also visiting Gene and Philly. 'Like a mother saying never play with knives. Art *is* play.'

Snapshots show us doing the sights in the snow: in front of the White House, the Capitol, the Lincoln Memorial: Gene, Alex, his girlfriend Julie, Paul and me, in different combinations depending on who took the picture. Philly stayed at home with the baby.

In the evenings Alex entertained us with jokes, quizzes and anecdotes – extraordinary stories about famous writers, historical characters, pop singers and baseball players. He wanted to know about the Royal Family and why Edward VIII had abdicated to marry Wallis Simpson. What was the secret of his obsession with this woman?

Alex was about to spend a year in London on a writer's fellowship. Julie was going with him.

'I wish you were going to be there,' he said. 'You could show us around.'

But we were going back to Africa.

We did meet up with Alex in London the following year, when we left Uganda and visited both sets of parents once more before setting off for Singapore. My mother invited Alex and Julie to Sunday lunch at the house in Streatham and I have a photo of a group walking on Tooting Bec Common that afternoon: my sister and the man who had just become her first husband, Alex and Julie, Paul and, contented in his pram, Marcel, who at three months was coping better than I was with intercontinental travel.

At some point during the years we spent in Singapore, Alex and Paul fell out. The quarrel was conducted entirely by letter. It started because Paul was dilatory about buying an opal ring for Alex's new girlfriend. (Julie was out of the picture by now.) Angry words were written and read, then the letters stopped. After a while they resumed without explanation and by the time we left Singapore, Alex and Paul were friends again.

Both brothers were writers. Alex was more academic and quirky, Paul far more prolific. In 1972, by which time Paul had published *Waldo*, *Fong and the Indians*, *Girls at Play* and *Jungle Lovers*, Alex published his first book, *Three Wogs*. The next year Paul spent a term (the fall semester) teaching at the University of Virginia in Charlottesville, where Alex also taught. When the boys and I flew out at Christmas, we were met at the airport by Alex, and his fiancée Linda, a beautiful student who shortly after threw him over and broke his heart. (He wrote about that in his next novel, *Darconville's Cat*.) For about a week we were constantly together, Alex and Linda, Paul and I, Marcel and Louis, who were four and two.

One night Louis wet the bed.

'My heart goes out to that little guy,' said Alex, though Louis had not been reprimanded and showed no sign of shame. As a child Alex had been scolded for bedwetting.

From 1975, for at least a decade, we saw Alex every summer on Cape Cod. His next girlfriend, Patricia, was a fisherman's daughter who excelled at playing charades. Then came Dale, who was married to a doctor (he wrote about her in *An Adultery*), then Cathy, a maths student. Women loved Alex. Those who left him did so because his elusiveness made them desperate.

Summers in the seventies and early eighties, when the children were small and Paul and Alex were friends, were the best times we had on Cape Cod. Paul's parents had retired to a house there and also owned a summer cottage which they let us use. Other members of the family came to stay. Gene and Philly, who now had three children, rented a cottage nearby. There was always a crowd. We played Scrabble, we played charades, we played tennis, we visited Provincetown, we went clamming, we hired cycles and rode round Martha's Vineyard. One year Alex had an operation on his nose. When the bandages came off it was very swollen and Louis, then five, said loudly, 'It looks like a great, big doorknob.' I froze. Alex laughed. He was indulgent with the children when they were small and they adored him because he played games as enthusiastically as they did.

Even in the good summers, though, there were times when Alex withdrew. Once I tried to talk to him about what was wrong.

'What is it, Alex? Have we upset you?'

'No, no, no, nothing.'

Alex stomped off to be alone. It was best to wait, knowing that sooner or later he would turn up and say, 'Hey, let's go to a movie.'

In the late seventies, Alex and Paul bought houses on the Cape within a few miles of each other. In 1983 Paul sold his house and bought a bigger one. We used to go to Alex's to play croquet and he would come to ours and organise ball games in the swimming pool. That had happened less frequently of late. Alex avoided us for longer and longer periods.

'Paul's a pain in the ass,' he told me eventually. 'He's so full of himself, he isn't fun anymore.'

'He doesn't mean to be a pain.'

'He can't carry his success lightly. He has no *sprezzatura*.'

It must have lodged in my mind that a disaffected brother could be a powerful ally. When I had been in despair about Paul's infatuation with the English teacher in Pennsylvania, Alex was the person to whom I turned, talking to him on the phone, this time endorsing his accusations: yes, Paul seemed to think he was omnipotent; success had gone to his head.

It felt good to have an ally in Paul's family, one who was willing to voice some of my own harsh thoughts. I had confided in Alex again, this year, after Paul left. We had exchanged phone calls and letters.

In the letter which I received on 18th December, Alex sent love and sympathy and made some critical observations about Paul. He recounted a conversation with the woman who served in a local grocery shop. 'Is Paul still married?' she had asked, as she wrapped his cheese. 'Only he was in here the other day with a dark-haired woman I haven't seen before.'

This information gnawed at me for a few hours. I knew I should keep it locked inside me but the urge to let it out was too sharp. I rang Paul and questioned him about this woman who seemed to be installed in our house on the Cape.

'I don't know what you're talking about. Who's been saying things about me?

'Mrs Treat in the West Barnstable store.'

A pause. 'It was Alex, wasn't it?' He sounded furious.

I knew I had done wrong and in the end I was punished, as wrongdoers are. Because of my phone call, Paul sent Alex a letter threatening to punch his reconstituted nose if he didn't keep it out of his business. Alex replied with equally violent words. They didn't see each other again for a long time. Alex wrote me a note, ending 'I want nothing more to do with either of you.'

Even before I received this final note, I knew it would be best not to see any of Paul's family while I was in America. I was too bitter and confused. It would put a strain on loyalties which were, in the end, not mine to claim. I had friends of my own there, I had my sons. Maybe, later, if things were resolved, these relationships could be restored.

Maybe I would never see any of these familiar faces again.

Saturday 22nd December

US. Arrived late. Taxi to hotel. Marcel was there.

⌒

Our flight had been delayed and it was already dark when the taxi pulled up outside a small hotel on 38th Street. Marcel appeared in the lit doorway. 'Mum, how are you? Good to see you. Lou, man! How are things? Want to go to a party later?' We ate dinner together, they shrugged on their coats, kissed me and left. I went to bed, envying their energy.

Sunday 23rd December

Got up early. (Louis had arrived home very late and was asleep) and walked to Central Park from 38th St. Saw people skating.

There is nothing like an early morning walk on a sunny day to remind you that life is worth living.

I watched people whirl and swish in the cold, clear air. Paul had brought me to the park at this time of year on my very first visit to New York, just after we were married, after we had met his family. We had traced its paths, arm in arm, and looked at the grey rocks among the shrubs. Later we had met his publisher for lunch and eaten bouillabaisse (we called it fishyssoise). Perhaps because I was pregnant, it made me sick.

Today I met Marcel and Louis at lunchtime. We ate big sandwiches then shopped in Macy's. In the evening we saw the film *The Bonfire of the Vanities*, which was not good. (*Seems racist to me* I noted in the diary.)

The day was reassuring. Even if I lost my relatives, I need not lose America. I could live here, if I wanted. I had never taken citizenship but I had an indefinite visa. I could buy a flat in New York. Get a job working for the UN. I liked America. I was glad I was here at the end of the year.

Chapter 15

Christmas 1990 and New Year 1991

Our plan was to take the bus to Sag Harbor, a trendy little seaside town on Long Island, to spend Christmas with my friend and her son. 'I know lots of people. There'll be plenty of parties,' she had assured me. This would be a different kind of Christmas. After all, it doesn't have to be several generations of one family, closeted together for the day, tearing at wrapping paper, eating turkey and Christmas pudding, pulling crackers, listening to the Queen's speech and playing silly games. In some circumstances that's the last thing you want.

'What did you say your name was?' It was Christmas Eve. The young woman next to me on the bus turned out to be a theatre critic. We chatted for the first part of the journey about plays to see in New York and London.

I said my name.

'How do you spell it?'

I spelt it. The intriguing foreign name with an x at the end which I had first seen on a lecture timetable at Makerere University. Improbably, it had been mine for 23 years.

'You're not related to ...?'

'Well, sort of ... Married. At least we were married. We've separated now.'

Perhaps she didn't hear the last bit.

'He's my favourite writer! Imagine being married to him! That's so exciting! Did you go on his trips with him?'

'Sometimes. Not often.'

I disengaged myself from the conversation by taking out a copy of *Wuthering Heights*. But I couldn't concentrate. Old Joseph was too tedious, with his incomprehensible speech. I looked out of the window at angular wooden buildings standing flat against a grey sky, a grey sea somewhere beyond. It was unmistakably New England. Memories and regrets whirled in my mind and I calmed myself by counting Christmases past.

Christmases 1942–64, the first 22 years of my life, were spent at my parents' house in Streatham, each one eagerly anticipated and over far too quickly. If I concentrated, I could picture details – the snowman with the grumpy face on the Christmas cake, the home-made paper-chains in the kitchen, the superior, shop-bought ones in the living room, which were stashed away in a suitcase at Twelfth Night. Sometimes grandparents and aunts and uncles were there. One year my mother and grandmother cooked a goose which filled the house with a rancid stink and was judged to have gone off. In 1946, the year my sister was born, beside the stocking Father Christmas had filled for me, was a short sock containing suitable presents for a baby: talcum powder, oil, soap and peeping out of the top, a green, china elephant, which I coveted. In 1962, my first year at university, I worked for the post office and delivered mail on Christmas morning. Twice it snowed. Maybe three times.

Christmas 1965 marked a big change. I was living in Nairobi, with a flatmate I called Annie, though her name was Anne, like mine. We had been invited to a Christmas party by a teacher at an agricultural college near Thomson's Falls, a hundred miles north. 'Bring your friends,' she said, as people did in those days, at that age, and about 50 young men and women arrived at the college on Christmas Eve with food, drink and sleeping bags. We slept uncomfortably on the floor, prepared and ate a large meal and then sat under the trees waiting our turn to telephone our families back home.

What could be better for someone stepping out into adulthood than Christmas under equatorial trees in a beautiful, newly independent country? The world was turning out to be brighter and more diverse than I had ever imagined.

It was my turn to go inside and phone.

'Mum! Dad! Rosamond! Happy Christmas! Wonderful. It's sunny, but not too hot. We're in the highlands. We're having a party. It's lovely here.'

Immediately after Christmas, a dozen of us travelled to Tanzania to climb Mount Kilimanjaro. It took three days to get up the mountain and on the final stretch I was overcome with altitude sickness and had to turn back, deeply disappointed not to reach the top. However, on the way up the mountain, before the oxygen got thin and the terrain grim, while we were still enjoying the views, the wild flowers, the fun of being together in the sunshine at the end of December, we met two Californians, John and Jim, Peace Corps volunteers, who taught in a remote village in Tanzania. Annie fell in love with John and conducted a long-distance affair throughout the following year.

And so for Christmas 1966, John visited Annie in Nairobi and brought Jim with him. By this time I was living in a hall of residence in Kampala, training to be a teacher, and I travelled 400 miles to join them, longing to see my old flat and some of my old friends. Annie cooked a ham, clattered the plates and got a bit fretful, as people do when they serve Christmas dinner.

That evening John, Jim, Annie and I took the night train to Mombasa, then hitchhiked northwards along the coast and rented a hut on a beach south of Malindi, where there were palm trees, white sands and a warm, blue sea. Space was limited and after a few beers Jim and I decided to share a bed. He was sexy and polite in a soft-spoken Californian way. We liked each other and when we returned to our different East African bases, we exchanged letters and arranged to meet again at Easter. But by that time the American in the white suit had delivered his 'Tarzan is an Expatriate' lecture and sneered at those of us who enjoyed 'having love affairs and doing a little good in a warm climate'. I had fallen in love.

It was easy to cable apologies to Jim and cancel our meeting. It was harder to work out how to rearrange the rest of my life. I had been given the posting I had asked for, at a rural school near Mount Kenya.

'But we must be together.' We were sitting in Paul's flat in Kampala which was littered with books, papers and parrot droppings. The parrot, named Kasuku, was eyeing me balefully from the back of the sofa.

'But I've only just started this teaching job. I have a two-year contract.'

'Break it.'

'I can't.'

'We can't spend the next two years 500 miles apart. It wouldn't work. It would be the end. Besides, I don't want to stay in Africa. I've had it.'

'I don't know what to do.'

Paul put his arms round me.

'I want you to marry me.'

As we kissed, jealous Kasuku ran along the back of the sofa and bit me on the arm.

Christmas 1967 was spent with Paul, in London, three weeks after our Kampala wedding. My parents, my sister and my sister's fiancé were there and it was another family Christmas, with the same decorations in the living room and the same grumpy snowman on the cake. Warmed by festivity, my parents relaxed with their new son-in-law. My father insisted we played a silly game. My mother teased Paul and told him he was handsome. Later in the afternoon, pleading jet lag, Paul and I went upstairs to the spare bedroom we had been allocated and Paul wanted to make love. I pushed him away, fearing we would be heard. He became angry. I became upset.

We had tried to compromise about our plans. Paul had agreed to stay at least another year in Africa. I had asked for a transfer from the school in Embu to one in Kampala so that we could be together and I could still teach.

'Impossible, I'm afraid,' said the administrator of the Teachers for East Africa scheme. 'We simply can't do that. Besides, if you marry, you will be breaking your contract. You will have to pay back all the money that's been spent on your training.'

'Give them the money.' Paul was angry. 'I'll pay.'

'But my work … I want to do what I came here to do.'

We argued fiercely and then made a new plan. I would resign, whatever the consequences. Later, when we were settled in Kampala, I would apply for a job in a local school. In the end the British government had waived the money I owed.

That plan was overturned when events in Rhodesia (Ian Smith began a series of illegal executions) sparked outrage around the world and demonstrators in Kampala attacked us in our car. I agreed to leave Africa. And so the next three Christmases – 1968 to 1970 – were in Singapore. There was a traditional meal at the house of Dennis and Madeleine Enright.

I bought a small silver tree at the Chinese Emporium and put it on our dining table to delight Marcel. But it didn't feel much like Christmas. And now we were a family, it was important that the rites were observed.

Adapting to marriage and motherhood was harder than I had expected. Paul took trips alone. He spent long hours at his desk. Sometimes I felt sad. In 1969 when I was pregnant with Louis, I shamed myself by bursting into tears when Bing Crosby sang 'White Christmas' on the radio.

There was happiness as well as disappointment in those Singapore years. Paul published *Fong and the Indians*, *Girls at Play* and *Jungle Lovers*; he gathered material for *Saint Jack*; a film option was taken on one of the books. I was intrigued by the students I taught at Nanyang University. We had two children we both adored. But the island was small and autocratic; it offered little scope for idealism. I was glad when the three years came to an end.

Christmas 1971 marked a new chapter in our life. We had just settled in England and spent it at my parents' house in Dorset. It was the best kind of family Christmas, spiced with trivial irritabilities. Marcel shocked my mother by asking for ketchup on his turkey and then annoyed both grandparents by saying sanctimoniously 'Never play with knives!' when my father cut himself as he prepared to carve. 'Grandpa wasn't *playing*,' said my mother reprovingly, while my father glared from under his paper hat and sucked his bloody thumb.

That was the start of a whole run of English Christmases, going right up to 1989, all the years we lived in England as a family. There were a few exceptions. Christmas 1972 was in Medford Massachusetts: the boys and I had joined Paul after his semester teaching in Virginia and we celebrated with his family. There was a nostalgic East African Christmas in 1984, when Paul and the boys met me at the end of my three months' research into the role of women in development. There was another American Christmas in 1987, at our house on Cape Cod: I cooked a turkey, Ann Marie brought lasagne and Louis made place cards for seventeen people. Was there also a Christmas at a ski-resort in the French Alps, or was that New Year? We did go on skiing holidays, several times, in France and then in Vermont.

But Christmas Day was mostly in England, at my parents' house in Dorset, our house in Catford, our house in Wandsworth, the Thames barge my sister lived on for a while or the house in Clapham to which she moved, with her second husband and their two sons. These Christmases followed the pattern set in my own childhood. Some years were good, others discontented. There was a sad Christmas in Catford in 1973, the year of Paul's *Great Railway Bazaar* journey. He didn't get back in time to spend it with us. It was as though he suspected that I had been unfaithful. (He had also been unfaithful, I found out later, with a journalist who interviewed him, but he said that didn't count.) I had told my lover that our affair had to end; I would confess to Paul and take the consequences. Meanwhile, feeling miserable and apprehensive, I did the usual things with mince pies and paper chains and stockings for the boys while a raucous group sang relentlessly on the radio, *I wish it could be Christmas every day-ay*. Paul arrived home shortly afterwards and his anger broke like a violent thunderstorm. He threatened to leave me; he would take the children away from me and go to America; he said unrepeatable things. Somehow we got through it and stayed together for another fifteen years, another fifteen Christmases.

Sometimes, when he was in a bad mood, Paul would complain how greedy and materialistic everyone was, and in a reversal of our usual roles (he was generally the one who enjoyed the trappings of success; I was the killjoy puritan) I defended the innocent pleasure of giving and receiving. One year when I was especially well organised and had decorated the house early, all the needles fell from the tree a week before Christmas Day. I consulted the family. 'Shall we buy another tree, or shall we give the money we would have spent on it to Oxfam and let the bare tree remind us of those less fortunate than ourselves?' 'Why can't we give money to Oxfam *and* get a new tree?' asked Marcel. I could think of no reason. We weren't poor, though we sometimes behaved as if we were.

Last Christmas, 1989, had been the worst, a travesty of all the others. We had drunk too much and barracked the Queen's speech; my parents had pursed their lips and pretended not to hear. We had played a disgusting game, competing to eat chocolate, and made my nephew cry. I didn't want any more Christmases like that.

'We're nearly there,' said the woman next to me. 'This is Sag Harbor.'

I shut my book. 'It was nice to meet you. I hope you enjoy the holiday.'

'It was nice to meet *you*!' she said. 'I loved *The Great Railway Bazaar*.'

Marcel, Louis and I got off the bus and were greeted enthusiastically by my friend, Tina, who took us shopping in the local mini market, where we bumped trolleys with Betty Friedan. Her book, *The Feminine Mystique*, had been among a handful which had made me aware of feminism and what it meant. Meeting her unexpectedly and being introduced seemed auspicious.

Tina's house was small, so she had booked us into a nearby hotel. We unpacked and put on our best clothes. There would be a party that evening, followed by Christmas dinner after the other guests left. It was dark and cold by the time we set out. I was carrying a Christmas pudding. Marcel and Louis walked on either side of me.

'Hey, Mum, this is all right,' said Marcel, taking my arm. 'We've got a party to go to, a Christmas pudding to take – it's OK.'

At the party, which was packed with writers, journalists and UN personnel, and during the meal afterwards with Tina and her son Ben, we talked about the war which was about to begin in the Gulf. Time was running out. Troops were gathering in vast numbers. Young men were being called up. Ben was 21; Marcel and Louis were 22 and 20. All of them had dual nationality and in theory could be required to fight by either Britain or America. And if they weren't, some other mothers' sons, at this very moment wiping turkey gravy from their chins, would go instead.

We exchanged gifts. Marcel and Louis gave me a black, crushed velvet scarf and a book – *Awakenings* by Oliver Sacks. I gave them sweaters I had bought in Macy's. Tina gave me a United Nations umbrella. I can't remember what we gave Tina and Ben.

Christmas continued. In the next couple of days we carried on partying, in Sag Harbor and then back in New York. There was plenty to eat and drink, plenty of friendly people to meet. Marcel and Louis were with me. Perhaps we could live like this for ever. *I wish it could be Christmas every day-ay!*

'Enough, Mum. No more being taken to parties, please. We're grown-up, remember.'

'Just dinner with the Penns. Then you can do your own thing. I think Dad's back from the Pacific. Why don't you visit him on the Cape?'

So on Thursday 27th December we had dinner with Arthur and Marilyn Penn and their three grown-up children at a Cajun restaurant on Sixth Avenue. This Arthur Penn is not the film-maker of that name. He was, perhaps still is, a wealthy lawyer. He and his wife loved art. I hope they still do. Paul's short story, *Altar Boy*, which became the first chapter in his book of autobiographical fiction, *My Secret History*, was commissioned by Marilyn as a 50th birthday present for Arthur. They used to take us out to dinner whenever we were in America and whenever they came to London too. On one occasion, in an attempt to reciprocate, Paul invited them to a meal at our London house with the film director Nic Roeg and his actress wife Theresa Russell, because Arthur was a fan of Roeg's. Paul used the evening as the basis of a story called *Burgess Slightly Foxed*, which appeared many years later in *The New Yorker*. Nic Roeg was transformed into Anthony Burgess who, in the story, drinks too much and becomes belligerent. Extra tension was added by the tetchy behaviour of the wife of the writer/host, and I objected to this portrayal of myself in a letter to *The New Yorker*. But at this time, two days after Christmas 1990, the story hadn't been written, though the evening that inspired it had come and gone. The Cajun restaurant had angel-lanterns hanging from the ceiling. We were given paper hats and whistles. After dinner we joined in a conga round the room. A farewell dance.

On Friday 28th December Marcel and Louis went to Cape Cod to see Paul, who had just flown in from Honolulu and I had lunch with Barbara, a friend from our time in Uganda; she had been married to Rajat Neogy, editor of *Transition* magazine. Their daughter, Tayu, was six months older than Marcel. We ate in a small restaurant near the Metropolitan Museum and talked about Africa, while snow fell softly in the dark streets outside. Barbara and Rajat had divorced some time ago; now Paul and I were separated.

'Please stay in touch,' she put her hand on my arm. 'As I get older, I value those who shared the past.'

By now I had seen all the people I knew in New York. Marcel and Louis had gone to the Cape. The city suddenly felt big and strange. It was a dangerous place, I recalled. People got mugged here all the time. I started glancing over my shoulder and clutching my handbag, as I did the rounds of museums and galleries.

On Saturday 29th December I went to the Guinness Records exhibition at the Empire State Building, the Museum of Modern Art and a play at the Lincoln Centre called *Six Degrees of Separation* (*very good*). The woman on the coach had recommended it.

On Sunday 30th December, after a visit to the Institute of Photography, I ate a tuna sandwich in a café and considered where to go next. The shops? The Guggenheim? Maybe the Frick; it was some time since I'd been there. I reached for my handbag to pay the bill.

'My handbag has gone.' Puzzled faces turned towards me. 'My purse. My purse has gone. It was on the back of the chair. It must have been stolen.'

'That's too bad. But it happens all the time here.' Other customers, unsurprised but sympathetic, rustled up $15 for me. I went back to my hotel, reported the incident to the police, cancelled all my credit cards and sat on the bed with my head in my hands, thinking lucidly. Passport: I must contact the embassy. Ticket: I must ring the airline. Money: American Express would arrange a new card. Recovering and coping, I felt a new energy.

The phone rang.

'Is this the lady who lost a black purse?'

It was the police. The bag with all its contents had been found in the Institute of Photography, beside the chair in the viewing room from which I had watched a video about the photojournalist Alfred Eisenstaedt.

'Thank you. What a relief. Where can I pick it up?'

Hot with embarrassment, at that moment I wished the bag had been lost forever.

It's the sort of incident my analyst would have enjoyed unravelling. Because I was worried about being mugged in New York, I created a situation in which my worst fears were realised without any mugger lifting a hand. Why was I so sure I would be mugged? Could it be because I already felt robbed, of my husband and much more besides? The full extent of my loss was only gradually becoming clear: the friends I would never see again, the relatives who could no longer treat me as one of the family; the status I had enjoyed as the wife of a successful writer. It would take time to tot up the damage. And the greatest loss could not be quantified. Something priceless had been stolen.

Collecting the bag from the police station took up much of the afternoon. After a solitary visit to the cinema to see Mel Gibson as Hamlet (*surprisingly good*) I returned to the hotel and leafed through my copy of *Wuthering Heights*, this time looking for the bits that would make me cry.

'*I cannot express it; but surely you and everybody have a notion that there is or should be an existence of yours beyond you. What were the use of my creation, if I were entirely contained here? … If all else perished, and he remained, I should still continue to be; and if all else remained, and he were annihilated, the universe would turn to a mighty stranger: I should not seem a part of it.*'

Emily Brontë, like Barbara Cartland, was inspired by the idea that a soul searches for its other half – and sometimes finds him. A romantic and dangerous notion that attracted me too. It seemed to explain how I felt. I was suffering the consequences of being separated from a part of myself; separated not by death or fate but by betrayal. No matter what I did, I could not feel whole.

On the morning of 31st December, Paul called me and said he was driving the boys back to New York. He wasn't sure what time they would arrive.

'I'd like to see you, if you're around.'

Would it have made a difference if I had agreed?

'I don't think I will be. It's my last day here. I have some shopping to do. And I want to go to Ellis Island.'

'Maybe we could meet up later …'

I was longing to see him, but not in this half-hearted way, as a second thought, a by-product. If he wanted to meet me, he must arrange it properly.

'I don't think so.'

I stayed out, taking the subway to Battery Park (I abandoned my plan to visit Ellis Island when I saw the queues for the ferry), then uptown to the shops, then tramping the streets, until I felt sure he would be on his way back to the Cape. I returned to the hotel. Marcel and Louis were there and Louis had a letter from Paul.

'I'll read it later. It looks long.'

I didn't want to spoil our last evening. Tomorrow Louis and I would fly back to England, leaving Marcel in America. Tonight we would enjoy a New Year's Eve dinner together, my sons and I, doing our best to ignore the minefield that lay ahead.

They were just at the start of their own adult lives, old enough to fight in a war. Were they old enough to understand? How could they understand when I didn't? I had always tried to be honest, to tell them the truth as I saw it, limited version though that might be. Now I didn't know the truth.

As we made our way to the restaurant, I resolved not to question them or put them on the spot. We always had plenty to talk about: the books we were reading, the films we had seen, the news of the day, the people we knew. Perhaps we didn't need to talk about the mess our family was in.

But how could we not talk about Paul? They had just spent two days with their father. And how could we talk about him, when they knew things I didn't know?

'How's Dad?' We were well into the meal. My caution had been diluted by wine. It felt safe.

'He's fine. He sent his love.'

'He really wanted to see you,' said Louis.

'I know. But I couldn't. Everything's too uncertain. I don't know where I am. And there's this other woman in the picture …'.

'She wasn't there.'

Relief. But I couldn't leave it at that. We were marching straight for the sign with the skull and crossbones.

'Not this time …?'

Eventually Marcel, anticipating orders, rushed desperately over the top, mentioning the letter he had written to Louis, which I had found – the story in which a young man intercepts a love fax from Honolulu to his father.

'I'm glad you read it. I wanted you to know.'

Swilling the wine about in his glass, nervously running his hand through his hair, he gave me the information I needed. This woman had been at the Theroux family Thanksgiving dinner held at Paul's house in November. (While I shivered in Pollok Park.) She had known Paul for a long time. She wore lots of make-up. She worked in public relations. She had helped plan Paul's trip in the Pacific. (No wonder he hadn't wanted me to travel there with him.) She could get discounts in hotels. She had designer luggage.

I listened without responding. Nothing new really. Just extra details, each one a deep stab with a very thin knife. At midnight we threw streamers and popped poppers. We walked back to the hotel and had a final drink. The boys had another party to go to. Marcel hugged me and said goodbye. He and his brother went out into 1991.

That was when I made the first telephone call of the new year.

Paul spluttered and made excuses and said how tired he was.

'This woman isn't important. I wanted to see you. I drove all the way to New York.'

'She broke up our marriage.'

'She isn't important.'

Rage pounded in my ears and a horrible noise came out of my mouth.

This is the last entry in the diary:

Monday 31st December

Avoided seeing Paul (who had insisted on driving Marcel and Louis back to NY — I'm sure because he wanted to see me). Went out to dinner with M and L. Saw in 1991 then totally pissed rang Paul and screamed abuse.

The next day, flying back, sitting next to Louis, I read the letter he had brought from Cape Cod and annotated it, inserting angry exclamations and cynical questions between words which seemed to have been written in a confused mixture of love and panic. He regarded losing me as the worst thing that had happened to him; it was mostly his fault; he wanted us to be reunited and felt he would never know real happiness unless we were. Yes, he'd had a woman friend during our separation; he had wanted to know what it was like to be with another woman without being unfaithful to me. He had proved to himself that he already had the best woman and family he could ever have had …

Oh yeah?

He outlined plans: a round-the-world trip; a return to the Pacific; a move to Hampstead; working on a joint project; building a house in Florida …

Chapter 16

That was the end …

That was the end of 1990 and the end of my diary – thank God, I thought as I wrote the final words: *rang Paul and screamed abuse*. 31st December. No more blank pages to fill. There might be bad times ahead but at least I wouldn't have to write about them.

There were some bad times over the next few years. There were more deceptions, more disappointments, more losses. Not all the losses were to do with Paul. Some of the people who appear in my diary, taken for granted as part of my life, have gone forever.

I would have been a fool not to realise by now that the marriage was over, that Paul loved someone else. Sometimes I *was* a fool, allowing myself to hope and my hopes to be dashed. I longed for a defining moment from which there could be no return, a pumpkin pie in the face like the one thrown by Meryl Streep at Jack Nicholson in the film *Heartburn*. I never quite managed to achieve anything as conclusive. Instead love died reluctantly by a thousand cuts.

None of the plans for the future outlined in Paul's letter to me at the end of December were taken further: there was no trip, no house hunting, no joint project.

Instead, in April, Louis flew to America to attend Paul's 50th birthday party. I wasn't invited.

Tomorrow is my husband's birthday.

Many old friends and the whole of Paul's family, except his brother Alex, were there. The party was hosted by Paul and the woman from Hawaii.

Only then, fifteen months after he had left, did I move his personal belongings from the house, reflecting angrily as I did so that he had slipped away leaving everything just as it was;

he had packed nothing, made no arrangements for mail to be forwarded, said no farewells to my family. I had hoped this meant that one day he would slip back, sit at his desk again, leaf through the books on his shelves again, visit my parents again, lie beside me in the brass-headed bed in the purple bedroom again, but I couldn't hang on to that belief when I pictured Paul and his family, our friends and our sons gathered round a table with another woman in my place.

He sent me a mug printed with the words: *Paul Theroux Half a Century of Progress*. I put it in a cupboard, but its presence disturbed me; I was sure *she* had designed it. One night, I came downstairs with a hammer, stood the mug on a sheet of newspaper and smashed it. I wrapped up the pieces and put them in the dustbin.

Leave me, O love, which reachest but to dust ...*

By a fortunate coincidence on 9th April 1991, the day before the birthday party, one of several good things happened to me. *Count your blessings*, we used to sing in Sunday School; later this advice struck me as foolish and cruel. But I have received blessings in my life, and this was one. I was offered a job at the BBC running the World Service Features and Arts unit. It was just the job for me, working with bright people, thinking up and making programmes about everything under the sun, broadcasting them to listeners in distant countries. It brought together my talents and interests; it made me look outwards at a world which I knew was large and varied. I did the job for six years,

* Sonnet by Sir Philip Sidney.

leaving when John Birt restructured the BBC in a way that disbanded my team. By that time I was ready to go. Like marriage, like life, those six years included rows and disappointments, but I remember more of the rewards. Getting this job meant I had to give up my plan to work abroad with VSO: by another coincidence I had at last been offered a suitable posting, in Sri Lanka helping with an educational communications project. It was a real alternative, but I had no hesitation in turning it down. My life was rooted in London now.

A second good thing was that I started a one-year evening course in couple counselling, learning how to understand relationships between two people. At the end of it I signed on to do a three-year Diploma course, with a view to becoming a counsellor myself, which I did, initially on a part-time voluntary basis. This meant I was engaged in a demanding job at the BBC during the day and studying or counselling three evenings a week. It was a full life and a fulfilling one, though it was a long time before the weight on my chest lifted and I felt whole again.

In an attempt to hasten this process I contacted the psychoanalyst we had both sought help from before (I hadn't been in touch with her since Paul left) and arranged to see her regularly.

The fourth big change took place much later. It had to do with the colleague who had left his wife for another woman. After our conversation in the BBC club, just before Christmas 1990, he eventually invited me to meet the woman he was living with and we all went out for a meal. I returned the invitation. We didn't see each other for a long time after that, though I heard from a mutual friend that the woman was terribly ill. One day, my colleague phoned and asked me to lunch the following Sunday. I mentioned this to the same mutual friend who sighed and said, 'Poor man. What shall we do for him?' 'Why? What's happened?' I realised even as I asked that his lover had died. Having lunch with me was part of his programme of recovery and survival. Over the next months we tentatively picked up some of the fragments of companionate life – shopping, cooking meals, going for drives in the country. Our sadness made us feel close.

Some time towards the end of 1992, Paul came to London to promote *The Happy Isles of Oceania*, the book about the trip arranged by the woman in Hawaii. (I haven't read it, but I gather there are references to me and how sad he felt about the separation, as if I had thrown him out.) We met for the first time in two and a half years. I told him there was someone else, hugged him and said goodbye.

A few months later he came over again and removed nearly all the paintings from the walls of the house, leaving their pale shapes on the tongue and groove panelling. He said he didn't want another man looking at his pictures. During the same visit he instructed a lawyer to draw up a petition, which I signed. An equal division of what we owned had already been agreed, without conflict. We were divorced on 18th July 1993. He also left a message written under my pine dining table, recalling the happy times we had spent around it and ending with the words, *This table is an altar. Never forget that love.* If you come to my house and lie on the floor with your head under the table, you can read the whole inscription, which he must have written in the posture of Michelangelo painting the roof of the Sistine Chapel.

On 18th November 1995, Paul re-married in Hawaii. Both our sons attended. I faxed my best wishes. The day before the marriage, I took the afternoon off work to attend the graduation ceremony for my counselling diploma. It took place in Tottenham Court Road, and on my way home I went into a shop to select a word processor, trying out several before I settled for this one, on which I wrote:

Tomorrow is my husband's wedding.
Tomorrow is ...
Tomorrow is ...

Postscript

Paul and I have now spent even more years with our present partners than the 22 we were together. Perhaps we learned from our mistakes. Perhaps we became less demanding as we grew older. Perhaps we chose more wisely. We live thousands of miles apart but have met up on friendly terms for family celebrations.

This account, written a few years after the events it describes, stayed in a drawer for a long time, during which I practised as a counsellor and listened to other people talk about the confusion and distress of troubled relationships. I shall never tell their stories, which have the seal of confidentiality, but now that I have retired, I can tell my own.

Anne Theroux 2021

Acknowledgements

My thanks to family, friends, colleagues and acquaintances whose companionship helped me on my journey. Some, but not all of you are mentioned in this memoir. Special thanks to my sister Rosamond and her family who were always there when I needed them, and to my husband, Michael Kaye, who encouraged me to publish.

And appreciation to Ellen Conlon, my editor at Icon Books, for assuring me that this story from the past has relevance today.